DEVELOPING LITERACY PROGRAMS FOR HOMELESS ADULTS

The Professional Practices in Adult Education and Human Resource Development Series explores issues and concerns of practitioners who work in the broad range of settings in adult and continuing education and human resource development.

The books are intended to provide information and strategies on how to make practice more effective for professionals and those they serve. They are written from a practical viewpoint and provide a forum for instructors, administrators, policy makers, counselors, trainers, managers, program and organizational developers, instructional designers, and other related professionals.

Editorial correspondence should be sent to the Editor-in-Chief:

Michael W. Galbraith
Temple University
335 Ritter Hall
Philadelphia, PA 19122

DEVELOPING LITERACY PROGRAMS FOR HOMELESS ADULTS

Joye A. Norris
Paddy Kennington

KRIEGER PUBLISHING COMPANY
MALABAR, FLORIDA
1992

Original Edition 1992

Printed and Published by
KRIEGER PUBLISHING COMPANY
KRIEGER DRIVE
MALABAR, FLORIDA 32950

Library of Congress Cataloging-In-Publication Data

Norris, Joye A.
    Developing literacy programs for homeless adults / Joye A. Norris,
Paddy Kennington.
        p.   cm.
    Includes bibliographical references (p. 103) and index.
    ISBN 0-89464-679-6 (acid-free paper) (cloth)
    ISBN 0-89464-794-6 (acid-free paper) (paperback)
    1. Literacy programs—United States. 2. Homeless persons—
Education—United States. I. Kennington, Paddy. II. Title.
LC151.N67 1992
374'.012 — dc20   92-19376
                                                      CIP

10   9   8   7   6   5   4   3   2

CONTENTS

Preface

Estimates on the number of homeless people in the United States range between 500,000 and 2 million (Interagency Council on the Homeless, 1990; National Coalition for the Homeless, 1991). The estimates pertaining to homeless children vary just as widely with figures going as high as half a million (Children's Defense Fund, 1991). Whatever the numbers, the problem is taking on dimensions unimaginable a decade ago, and growth in homelessness is expected to continue, particularly among women and children.

Literacy educators, through the Stewart B. McKinney Homeless Assistance Act, have been making a concerted effort to provide a wide range of basic skills training to homeless adults, that is, to those adults who do not have a fixed address and who live on the streets, in shelters, and in various transitional settings. Nationally, most efforts have been carried out through the Adult Basic Education (ABE) program, the largest federally funded literacy effort. ABE has a long history of reaching and serving disadvantaged adults (Hunter & Harman, 1979). It has an equally long history of developing approaches to literacy training that reflect the needs of learners. When the opportunity arose to provide programs for homeless adults, ABE practitioners joined other educators and literally headed for the streets.

Bolstered by special funding that included support service dollars, the ABE instructors took what they had already been doing in adult literacy classes right into shelters, soup kitchens, welfare motels and hotels, day labor pickup sites, side-walks, and storefronts. But their past experiences, training programs, and curriculum materials immediately fell far short of the challenge. Program after program reported barriers to instruction not previously seen in such variety or magnitude (U.S. Department of Education, 1990b). "Flexibility" was re-defined and "alternative approaches" took on new meaning as well. Had there been a drawing board, the ABE practitioners would have returned to it.

This book, in a sense, serves as that drawing board for providers of literacy education for homeless adults. Literacy program administrators, coordinators, instructors, and volunteers will benefit from this volume as they design and imple-ment education initiatives. While primary literacy focus in this text is through ABE, all literacy providers will find strategies to assist them. Shelter providers and volunteers, as well as community service organizations in general, will find valuable insights into educational barriers and opportunities.

Other beneficiaries include library administrators, many of whom are finding themselves on the cutting edge of both literacy education and services to the homeless. Vocational program planners and job placement professionals will benefit from this volume as they consider steps to reach and assist homeless adults. Community action organizations seeking to move adults along a continuum toward more independence will learn what role literacy education may play in that en-deavor. Students of both literacy and homelessness will benefit from this volume's examination of the breadth and scope of literacy education and its application to an especially trauma-tized segment of our society. Agency staff dealing with other issues of homelessness, including poverty, health, transporta-tion, and housing, should find value in the considerations ex-pressed in this volume.

Chapter 1 takes the reader directly into the realities of working in the world of homelessness. Barriers to instruction including the physical and psychological environment where people live are described. Shelter and literacy program rules and regulations are discussed as they relate to impeding educational progress. Finally, the trauma of homelessness itself is reviewed as it relates to the homeless adult as a learner.

How literacy education, particularly through ABE, fits into the overall support service system for homeless adults is discussed in Chapter 2. The definition and roles of literacy education with this population continue to evolve. Some of these roles are predictable and others, a complete surprise. Chapter 3 takes a deeper look at the homeless adult as an adult learner. Some principles of adult learning are reviewed in relation to their applications to homeless adult education.

Working as an instructor for homeless literacy projects requires "showing respect" and "relating to learners." Yet as teacher characteristics, however necessary, these qualities are not sufficient. Strong and wide-ranging instructional skills are equally important. Chapter 4 contains guidelines for ABE practitioners as they send well-intentioned instructors into very difficult situations.

Chapter 5 offers readers program design goals that have evolved since the initiation of the first McKinney-sponsored education programs. These goals are representative of accumulated trials and errors and resulting perspectives on what literacy education for homeless adults can be. The goals are followed in Chapter 6 by program design models that can provide starting places for administrators of new literacy projects for homeless adults. A frame of reference for understanding current practices is included for seasoned administrators.

Program planning strategies and evaluation possibilities are discussed in Chapter 7. Ideas of learner-centered adult educators and literacy researchers are incorporated into the evaluation strategies. Finally, issues and implications for the future are addressed in Chapter 8. Emphasis is placed on the next steps toward serving homeless adults and making a difference in ending homelessness in the United States.

One of the most exciting aspects of serving homeless adults through adult basic education has been the requirement to maintain flexibility in thinking and in practices. The homeless literacy projects have in many ways served as an incubator for fresh ideas about literacy education. The authors hope readers of this volume will use it not only to help define current practice but to spin off ever more program models, curriculum approaches, and evaluation methods. Serving homeless adults requires constant program review and change of practices which is, overall, a healthy turn of events for adult basic education.

The Authors

Joye A. Norris is the coordinator of the Homeless Literacy Project at Wake Technical Community College in Raleigh, North Carolina. She has guided the development of a comprehensive basic skills program involving several shelters and hundreds of homeless adults. In response to the unique circumstances and learning needs of the homeless learners, Dr. Norris oversaw the development of the Lifeskills for the Homeless Curriculum, now in use nationally. She was the Program Chairperson for the Second National Conference on Adult Education for the Homeless held in Greensboro, North Carolina, in March 1992. By building upon existing community resources and developing innovative approaches to both shelter and community based programs, the Wake Tech program is currently serving several hundred homeless adults each year in a variety of ways.

After serving as a public school instructor, a vocational counselor, and a teacher of adults in a college transfer program, Dr. Norris earned her doctorate in Counselor Education from North Carolina State University, receiving her Ed.D. in May 1989. By that time, she had turned her attention to literacy instruction and issues, and she focused her dissertation research on adult basic education. Prior to her appointment as coordinator for the homeless literacy project, Dr. Norris served for two years as a literacy instructor, working with a broad range of students in diverse settings.

In addition to her work with homeless adults, Dr. Norris

is also the owner of Triangle Learning Design, and she provides training to literacy instructors, Cooperative Extension Service agents and paraprofessionals, health educators, and others working with hard to reach populations. She is an experienced developer of grant proposals and offers training in this area as well. Currently, Dr. Norris is studying and writing about the power of partnerships in meeting the tremendous needs of educationally and economically disadvantaged members of our society.

Paddy A. Kennington is presently pursuing a doctoral degree in Counselor Education at North Carolina State University in Raleigh, North Carolina. She is a recent recipient of a Patricia Roberts Harris graduate fellowship. Ms. Kennington has served as Dr. Norris's assistant in the Homeless Literacy Project at Wake Technical Community College for the past two years.

Before coming to North Carolina in 1989, Ms. Kennington worked as a community activist and organizer on issues of homelessness in Savannah, Georgia. She organized and directed a food bank, night shelter, and soup kitchen. She was also active in groups that organized health care services and a local homeless coalition in Savannah. In this capacity, Ms. Kennington managed public relations and fundraising campaigns and public awareness efforts while advocating for homeless people and the organizations that serve them. She also worked with homeless advocates in Savannah and Atlanta, Georgia, in an effort to influence local and state legislation and policies.

Ms. Kennington received a B.S. (1969) in secondary school and science education from Valdosta State College, Valdosta, Georgia. She received a B.S. (1972) in medical technology and an M.Ed. (1980) in counseling and psychology from Georgia State University in Atlanta, Georgia. Ms. Kennington completed a graduate certificate in spiritual direction in 1989 from Washington Theological Union, Silver Spring, Maryland. Her articles on prayer and spiritual direction have appeared in *Review for Religious*, *The Witness*, *The Friends Journal*, and *Living Prayer*.

CHAPTER 1

Barriers to Instruction When Serving Homeless Adults

Literacy programs for homeless people must adapt to both student needs and their existing environmental circumstances while maintaining the integrity of literacy instruction. Nationally, most efforts to provide basic skills remediation and literacy training are based in shelters. Typical class sites not in shelters include soup kitchens, libraries, local schools, and nearby churches. Less typical are classes near day labor pickup spots or at the racetrack.

"Going where the homeless are" has been a mainstay credo of homeless literacy projects, but it has also resulted in a range of difficulties. These difficulties will be examined in this chapter through the filter, so to speak, of offering instruction. Categories of barriers include those related to the shelter environment, shelter rules and regulations, the circumstances of homeless adults, and literacy program requirements.

THE SHELTER ENVIRONMENT

A broad continuum of public to private and temporary to permanent characteristics define the present system of sheltering homeless people in America (Rivlin & Imbimbo, 1989). The broadest framework for defining the sheltering system ranges through three tiers: emergency shelter, transitional shelter, and permanent housing (Stoner, 1989). There is no uniform shelter "franchise," and conditions vary markedly from shelter to shelter within each city.

A big warehouse filled with 140 cots and staffed by church volunteers will present different challenges to instruction than the stately old home that has been converted into transitional housing for homeless families. Some transitional housing is in the form of apartments, in stark contrast to the wooden bunk beds stacked three-high in the basement of a downtown church. Barriers or situations that serve to deter instruction are described henceforth as representative samples ranging from the understated to the overstated.

A typical emergency shelter housing men and/or women without children can be too noisy, too hot, and too crowded for almost any learning activity. If the shelter operators provide meals, the evening hour can be hectic while people are being fed and clean-up activities are completed. The presence of numerous volunteers, while a heartening sight, also contributes to the overall commotion. In smaller shelters, residents may have few places to go after dinner except to high-volume television areas or makeshift lounges. Shelter residents may choose to talk loudly, play music, and talk on the phone, activities which are completely expected but which are also barriers to instruction in cramped spaces. The national habit of serving as many homeless people as possible for the fewest dollars, coupled with increasing numbers of homeless people, ensures continuing distractions in shelters (Stoner, 1989).

Instructional space in a shelter setting may be at a premium and very likely inadequate for any kind of instruction. Instructors may literally teach off an ironing board or a console television top. Instructors would likely be carrying all instructional materials in the trunk of a car, including audiovisual equipment. Cold weather or emergencies may result in a designated instructional space being used instead for extra beds. When the only teaching space available is within the confines of residents' rooms, interruptions are a way of life. Ironically, though, a quiet room set off from most shelter activities can become an instructional liability. It can cut the instructor off from shelter activities and thus not allow shelter residents to develop trust or comfort in the program.

Many shelters do have children present, often with no system of child care available. In already crowded conditions, the addition of children worsens a trying situation. Even when child care is available, homeless parents are often reluctant to entrust their children to the care of strangers. Fear of family disintegration and the intervention of social workers who might place their children in foster care prompts many homeless parents to cling to their children (Hagen, 1987; Johnson & Kreuger, 1989; McChesney, 1990). Anxious parents sometimes keep small children with them as a kind of security blanket. Others do not believe anyone else can manage their pre-school children (Dail, 1990).

The shelter setting often throws people with all kinds of physical, mental, and emotional difficulties into the same space (Johnson & Kreuger, 1989). An organizational one-size-fits-all mentality, made necessary by limited space and finances, can result in frustration with noisy, boisterous guests, emotional outbreaks, medically-related seizures, arguments, and tense scenes. Visits from members of local police departments are not unusual in some situations, particularly if some residents have consumed alcohol before arriving or have brought a previous argument into the shelter with them.

Shelters and soup kitchens are often housed in deteriorating buildings in dilapidated neighborhoods where unused, unwanted property is available more cheaply. Despite the best efforts of shelter or soup kitchen staff and police diligence, areas surrounding the shelters are often riddled with crime and violence. Concerns for safety of instructors coming and going in evening hours is a legitimate problem in many areas of the country.

In spacious or more homelike settings, factors that may hamper instruction are also present. Constant activity makes instruction a challenge. Without a separate room for instruction, teachers will often find themselves literally in peoples' kitchens and living rooms, and not everyone present is a student! The presence of additional families waiting out on the street while sleeping in the family car adds to the intensity of the situation. Day shelter sites are no exception in presenting barriers. Depending upon shelter management and philosophy, instructors may be dealing with similar issues, exacerbated by lack of adequate staff, large crowds in the winter, people sleeping off the effects of alcohol or because they are seriously ill, and inadequate furnishings. A heavy reliance on volunteers at all kinds of shelters sometimes means a sacrifice in perceived authority figures and added stress for an instructor who may be looked upon as the only available person in charge.

SHELTER RULES AND PROGRAM REQUIREMENTS

Variations on rules and program requirements are as broad as the types and definitions of shelters. Three types of regulations that may prove troublesome to literacy projects are common across the sheltering spectrum: hours of operation, length of stay, and individual program demands.

Depending upon the type of shelter, the hours of operation factor in considerably when designing instruction. A typical, winter-weather emergency shelter may not open until 7:00 p.m. at night. Clients must often depart the premises by 6:00 a.m. in the morning. If the only instructional time available is in the late evening, then instruction will compete against fatigue and, often, will lose. Some shelter programs also have strict work requirements which further limit access to learners.

The early morning departure requirement will likely have some shelter guests more concerned with adequate sleep than with any kind of instruction. In one case, a local literacy project was given the hour and a half between a 6:30 a.m. wake-up call and an 8:00 a.m. shelter departure time for instructional purposes, competing with breakfast and the usual activities expected in people's mornings. Dinner, if provided, may have to be served late in the evening, and any kind of instruction must follow it. Instructors may be reluctant to work such late hours.

Nearly every homeless shelter, from the most temporary to the more transitional, has limitations on length of stay. A family may get a week or two; a single male may get a certain number of nights per month; and a battered woman may have six weeks before she has to find a place of her own. In one southern city, the six emergency shelters are probably typical. One shelter allows men to sleep in its transient beds one night out of three. In another shelter, men may stay one or two nights, unless they are employed and are then eligible for nine nights (Hollingsworth et al., 1990). In many instances, homeless adults rotate in and out of several area shelters. Setting educational goals—or goals of any other kind—can be extremely difficult under these circumstances.

Shelter providers are usually operating on a particular philosophy and sometimes on a total program format. Men allowed to sleep at a certain shelter may be required to attend a nightly church service after dinner. Instruction would then be limited to after church hours, again moving the educational enterprise late into the night. Attendance may be required at substance abuse programs or parenting classes at another shelter. The stipulation to work at the shelter can also limit instructional time. Sometimes these requirements are directly related to the larger shelter enterprise which supports itself partly through the labors of residents, and these requirements are often inflexible.

Shelters for battered women may be much more than "shelters." Typically, residents are participants in a broader program of counseling, parenting, and general lifeskills activities. These requirements will have first priority with shelter program directors. Another common occurrence that affects instruction is the possibility that a learner has been ejected from the shelter for an infraction of a rule. That person may not be allowed to return for quite some time, if ever.

In many shelters across the country, activities other than sheltering and feeding are taking place. Enrichment activities such as art, parenting, and nutrition classes may already be occurring at these shelters. Other common activities such as clothing distributions, visits from a health clinic nurse or case manager or Social Security representative, footwashings, and storytelling may be taking place. In fact, most studies of the needs of homeless adults and families stress the urgency for comprehensive services (Cohen, 1989; Hagen, 1987; Hutchison, Searight, & Stretch, 1986; Ropers, 1988; Sosin & Grossman, 1991; Walsh, 1990; Wood, Valdez, Hayashi, & Shen, 1990).

Not all education programs are based at shelters. In some

instances, program developers may try to establish educational activities at sites away from the shelters, but that does not remove all barriers. Potential learners must be available at certain times and locations in order to catch a bus or van. Sudden work opportunities may divert the learner from boarding the bus in the first place. Fear of unknown sites and people may deter participation, particularly for non-English-speaking persons, the mentally ill, or battered women. Most sites away from shelters have to provide child care and transportation, both very expensive and paperwork-entangled activities.

Instructors located away from shelter locations do not have the opportunity to mingle with residents and develop a trusting relationship or an ease of presence that may be required if learners are going to participate. Also, the best developed plans for non-shelter site programs will not stand up to shelter operator indifference to the effort. Adjustments in operating hours or exceptions to the rules may not be forthcoming if shelter provider support is lackluster. Some other educational programs are offered literally where homeless people are standing, eating, or working. The circumstances can be extraordinarily troublesome and finding instructors willing to teach basic skills at a day labor pickup site or a race track is a feat in itself!

ADULT LEARNERS IN HOMELESS SETTINGS

Homeless persons bring to any learning process a constant and pervasive awareness of their immediate survival needs (Fried, 1963). Any individual who has lost a stable environment experiences some degree of anxiety, apprehension, and frustration, even when extended stays in transitional housing are an option (Kozol, 1988). For educators to go into homeless shelters expecting to find learners anxious to enroll in programs is often to be very naïve. It is equally unrealistic to assume that homeless adults and shelter providers view acquisition of literacy skills as a priority issue. In general, literacy skills are not a priority issue for millions of Americans who are considered by some standards to be in need of the training, as Beder and Valentine (1987) learned in their study of nonparticipation in literacy programs.

Hunter and Harman (1979) described four groups of literacy students, beginning with the group most closely representing the cultural mainstream value on education. These adults "respond readily to opportunities to learn and expect to fit in a classroom approach" (p. 111). While adults meeting this description may be found in homeless shelters, they are certainly the minority. Yet even the homeless adult learner who does express an interest in further education poses challenges to instruction: fatigue and distraction, mental and physical illness, substance abuse, and trauma and gender issues. Each of these will be discussed briefly.

The daily stress and crisis atmosphere of the streets, social service agencies, soup kitchens, and shelters naturally result in the learner's struggle to focus on anything, let alone learning. Day labor jobs in the construction and fast food industries are physically demanding. Exhaustion and hunger are of prime concern. People under such pressure may be inclined to ask an instructor, "Can't you just leave the book?" The difficulties are exacerbated by previously mentioned shelter operating hours and the late dinner hour. Adding to the exhaustion for some adults is the responsibility for child care. Homeless adults typically must take their children with them as they seek assistance and employment. Once sleep is possible, it may be difficult when children are anxious or upset about their surroundings.

Shelter environments have already been discussed in terms of the barriers to instruction. For the homeless adult, distractions go beyond the surroundings. The potential learner may not be able to concentrate on basic skills, or any other kind of skills, when the necessity of finding another place to stay looms in the immediate future. An instructor at a battered women's shelter noted that she could tell at what stage of the six-week program people were in by their attentiveness during instruction. The newest residents, she said, clearly could not focus on anything or, in some cases, even speak. Those nearing the end of their stay were visibly anxious about finding an apartment. Only those in the middle of their stay seemed to be really involved in learning.

Homeless people's health problems, both mental and physical, tend to go untreated until they worsen, and thus interfere with other activities. Wright and Weber (1987) note that one in eight homeless adults suffers from chronically poor physical health. Homeless adults often endure untreated injuries because they do not have access to treatment or would lose a day of work if they should seek care. In addition to physical health problems, loneliness and absence of family members affect the learner. The women in Dail's (1990) study of homeless families report a severe perceived social isolation and alienation and an inability to trust anyone at any time. While researchers caution practitioners not to assume all homeless people are socially isolated (Shinn, Knickman, & Weitzman, 1991), affiliations appear to diminish significantly as homelessness is protracted (Goodman, Saxe, & Harvey, 1991).

Substance abusing shelter residents may have problems focusing on learning. While many shelter programs require sobriety as a condition of residence, others do not. The instructor's sober learner one night may be back another night, still desiring instruction but clearly under the influence of alcohol. Mentally ill residents may or may not be taking prescribed medications, with either situation affecting learning potential. Suspected but often undiagnosed learning disabilities present an additional barrier to concentration. In some instances, an obstacle to even minimal participation in educational activities is a generalized passivity, brought on by lengthy experience with having no control over one's life (Goodman, Saxe, & Harvey, 1991).

An increasing number of non-English-speaking migrant or seasonal farmworkers are making their way to soup kitchens and shelters. The language barrier, coupled with fear of authorities, makes learning extremely difficult. Even when bilingual instructors are provided, conditions are challenging. The paperwork requirements of publicly funded programs are particularly burdensome for homeless adults whose status in this country is questionable.

Also, the language needs are so great for the non-English speaker that it would be difficult to see any progress in short periods of time. One instructor working with Spanish-speaking men, many of whom were residing under a local bridge, was asked to bring maps to the classroom. She assumed her students were referring to street maps of the immediate area. What they really wanted, however, was a map of the United States because they had absolutely no idea where they were.

The homeless adult may resist working in groups and demonstrate frustration and distraction in such cases. In the loss of home, many people suffer a sense of dislocation from their usual group identities (Fried, 1963). Also, little energy is left to apply to group interaction demands, even if one wanted to participate. Russell (1988) notes that none of the homeless women, when interviewed, "exhibited a high energy level although many women . . . were young and seemingly healthy" (p. 196). Homeless people can, according to Goodman and others (1991), "lose faith in their ability to care for themselves and in the willingness of others to help them, and may develop an abiding sense of mistrust of others" (p. 1221).

Shelters housing men and women create additional barriers to learning when instruction is offered to both groups together. Women may be especially reluctant to indicate an interest in learning when men are present. They may choose to remain uninvolved even when they might actually be interested. Russell (1988) based her research on the differences between homeless men and women, and she found the differences to be substantial. The women in her study often felt they had failed in their role of mother and homemaker. The woman's shame resulting from being homeless perhaps would be compounded if she were seen learning to read and write.

In one shelter situation, the instructor felt very discouraged that women were not participating in any learning activities. The shelter housed 25 men and 10 women, but only the men were involved in instruction. One evening, Linda, a poet, asked to speak to the instructor privately, "in the office." The office turned out to be the ladies' restroom. The instructor reported that within a few minutes, four women plus herself were crowded into the restroom, engaging in conversation about Linda's poetry and about their own dreams. It was the first time the women had ever displayed an interest in instructional activities. And it was the first time they had had private space away from the men.

LITERACY PROGRAM REQUIREMENTS

Ironically, a significant barrier to instruction may be the literacy program itself. Stewart B. McKinney funds for statewide literacy initiatives have been channeled through state education agencies (U.S. Department of Education, 1989). A majority of these McKinney-funded efforts have taken form through adult basic education programs. Tension has resulted because of accountability requirements and the realities of providing educational opportunities to homeless adults. Concerns include class setup procedures, attendance requirements, and assessment policies. An additional barrier is in the form of tradition: 25 years of educational approaches and materials that may not be appropriate for homeless adults.

The language of publicly run literacy programs such as ABE symbolizes the inevitable strain between administrative demands and homeless adult education. Enrollment forms, rosters, attendance sheets, permanent record and student progress cards are examples of that language. The very idea of "enrollment" can be a problem. The learner is asked to fill out forms; provide a signature in one or two places; provide an address, telephone number, employer name, last school attended, highest grade completed, birthdate, and referral source. Results include a range from resistance to comply to a collection of informative and questionable data. The difficulties are especially acute when the learners neither speak English nor desire to provide the information even if they had it. Women staying in shelters for battered women are rightfully reluctant to give such detailed information on official forms.

Instructors often view the necessity to actually enroll learners as an unfortunate phenomena that has the effect of driving away participants. In shelter situations, it may take quite some time before an instructor develops a trusting relationship with shelter residents, let alone manage detailed paperwork. Instructors in the field often report a learner's refusal to comply with requests for signatures, birthdates, and Social Security numbers. The last item poses unique headaches. Many homeless adults do not have a Social Security number, do not remember it, or fill in a false number. The latter situation causes great problems when a program has existed long enough to start seeing former participants return to the shelter class.

Minimum attendance requirements come into play if the sponsoring agency must have a certain number of student contact hours to justify hiring the instructor. Attendance minimums may pose the greatest barrier of all to successful homeless literacy projects, since they have the potential of eliminating the program's ability to weather up and down attendance that is inevitable in homeless situations. Even when instructors are supported through special funds outside regular literacy budgets, relatively low attendance or participation makes the program difficult to justify.

Skills assessment procedures are an integral part of publicly funded and administered literacy programs, and are generally required. Entering ABE literacy students are tested for reading and math grade level equivalents or for functional literacy scores. These results are part of the record and part of the ongoing measurement of program success. Assessment in a homeless shelter or nearby location becomes a challenge if the instructors must adhere to the same requirements.

It isn't unusual for instructors to spend just one or two hours with a learner, and the wisdom of using that time for assessment procedures becomes questionable. The testing requirement might also turn potential learners away just as it does in the broader literacy efforts (U.S. Department of Education, 1992). The shelters are usually very public places filled with people who are strangers to each other, and interest in taking tests is understandably minimal. If the tenure in a shelter environment is expected to be longer than a few days, and if the learner desires it, more formal assessment makes sense.

Basic skills instruction has been offered through federally supported adult basic education programs since 1966, and, in many ways, few instructional changes have been made. Instruction by and large is discrete-skills oriented and ultimately directed toward the attainment of academic credentials. Curriculum materials have been designed primarily on an academic model. Implicit in the approach has been that academic skills are transferable to other life areas and interests. When the traditional approach has been applied to homeless adult learners, however, considerable obstacles have been encountered. Program directors and instructors used to going into off-campus locations and setting up classes, using typical assessment and prepackaged instructional materials, quickly learned that "traditional" in homeless shelters would take on new meaning.

The range of surprises can be very broad. In one instance, a carefully planned class was set up at an urban mission. The instructor had stocked the mission library with typical reading, math, and writing books, covering reading levels from nonreader to GED preparation. In the teacher's box were traditional assessment materials and worksheets. After the instructor had decided that no one was going to join the class, a young man finally came to the library door with a notebook and pencil in hand. He looked at the instructor and asked, "Is this where I can get help reviewing my trigonometry?"

In another instance, a shelter resident had asked the on-site instructor where a particular office was located in the city. As the two of them searched the city map for the correct street, the young woman and mother of two children asked, "Can you show me what you are doing? I've never known how to find anything on a map, and I don't understand what you're saying." Assumptions about knowledge levels and too heavy a reliance on the trappings of traditional literacy education approaches can prevent educators from being the change agents they desire to be.

DISCUSSION

A staff member at a woman's shelter in the eastern United States described the lack of privacy and constant commotion at the shelter. "Being in this space," she said, "would be like sitting in a train station at rush hour, every hour of every day" (Imbimbo & Pfeffer, 1987). Educators, eager to serve homeless adults and willing to go the extra mile, have brought their efforts to previously uncharted territory and have probably felt that they too were on that train.

The shelter environments have made providing instruction remarkably trying. Shelter rules and requirements have been mixed blessings. The homeless adults themselves are in traumatic circumstances and may find any additional activity other than surviving each day just too taxing. Finally, educators have sometimes been restrained by their own program requirements which are sensible in more mainstream situations but barriers when serving the homeless.

What roles can literacy education play under these circumstances? Given the crisis nature of homelessness, is a program of basic skills remediation appropriate? Can literacy training really make a difference in homeless people's lives? These questions will be examined in the following chapter.

CHAPTER 2

The Meaning and Role of Literacy Education for Homeless Adults

Defining literacy education for homeless adults is like writing one's job description after having held the job for three years. The description reflects what one has made of the position. In July, 1988, adult educators set out to provide basic skills remediation and literacy training to homeless adults in their communities. Two critical assumptions preceding their efforts were that homeless adults needed such training and that adult educators would know how to provide it. Neither assumption appeared off base. Homelessness is associated with poverty and unemployment. Federal literacy efforts have historically come from the premise that literacy and job training are palliatives for both conditions.

The Stewart B. McKinney Homeless Assistance Act (U.S. Department of Education, 1988) provided for state literacy initiatives that would develop the literacy training. The McKinney Act utilized definitions of literacy training that are taken nearly verbatim from those that public literacy practitioners and administrators have been using for years. Basic skills remediation and literacy training were defined as:

> Adult education for homeless adults whose inability to speak, read, or write the English language constitutes a substantial impairment of their ability to get or retain employment commensurate with their real ability, which is designed to help eliminate such inability and raise the level of education of those individuals with a view to making them less likely to become dependent on others, to improving their ability to benefit from occupational

training and otherwise increasing their opportunities for more productive and profitable employment and to making them better able to meet their adult responsibilities (U.S. Department of Education, 1988). (p. 1)

Through the State Literacy Initiatives (Title VII-A, Section 702, U.S. Department of Education, 1988) funds were distributed to both public, nonprofit, and community-based organizations. In 1989, 26 of the 29 states receiving the federal funds channeled dollars through public agencies exclusively or through a combination of public and nonprofit organizations (U.S. Department of Education, 1990b). Thus, the majority of initial efforts were carried out within ABE programs that had already been providing literacy education to adults. The steps were in place to carry traditional literacy programs into homeless shelters, soup kitchens, and other homeless-oriented environments. In hindsight, it makes sense that the first educators arrived on the scene with traditional approaches and materials. It also makes sense in hindsight that early reports from the field indicated trouble.

Barriers to instruction were numerous and compelling. Among the obstacles reported to federal administrators were "transient nature of students," "lack of shelter support," "urgent priorities other than education," "continuing substance abuse," "lack of interest," and "poor self esteem" (U.S. Department of Education, 1989). Educators had assumed that homeless adults would be eager to participate in classes and would have time to accomplish educational objectives. The realities were different. Many of the homeless adults were high school graduates and, in some cases, college graduates. Many of those who were lacking in basic skills lived up to Fox's (1986) idea about undereducated adults in general: "People tend to want specific strategies to deal with specific problems, not generalized assistance in learning to encode and decode written language" (p. 1).

Educators also discovered what Hunter and Harman (1979) proposed would be the case: "Experience in other countries suggests that literacy is seldom a first priority among those who themselves are unlettered" (p. 8). The authors believed that when given the chance to describe their own needs, people are "more likely to stress first their economic problems, followed by such personal concerns as family living, child care, health, and nutrition" (p. 8).

Nearly ten years later, Russell (1988), in her study of homeless women in Baltimore, Maryland, found that the women wanted first a home, then their children returned, and finally their health. Other big concerns were food and physical appearance. Literacy skills were not mentioned. The stigma of illiteracy, combined with the stress of homelessness, likely deterred many adults from revealing their basic skills status (Beder, 1991). In a sense then, the early teachers went uninvited into people's homes, no matter how temporary those homes were, with programs that people hadn't asked for, and with little, if any, prior knowledge of the complexities of homelessness.

From the initial discoveries and program attempts, several roles for literacy education in serving the homeless have evolved. An examination of these roles begins with what was anticipated at the outset: the provisions of basic reading, writing, and math skills. Other roles include providing preparation for high school credentials, enhancing lifeskills, and assisting with transactional activities. But broader purposes and roles for literacy education have been revealed and, along with more traditional roles, will be reviewed in the following chapter.

THE PROVISION OF BASIC READING, WRITING, AND MATH INSTRUCTION

Very little of the sociological and psychological literature about homeless adults refers to illiteracy as a significant variable in the understanding of homelessness (Bassuk, 1990). Assessments that test functional competencies have been questioned by literacy professionals who believe the test items are irrelevant to people's actual lives (Kazemek, 1983). Nevertheless, available data indicates that some adults who are illiterate or have very poor literacy skills, including some high school graduates, exist in shelter settings. The possibilities of offering basic skills remediation certainly exist in establishments frequented by homeless adults.

Eleven agencies serving homeless populations in California were involved in a systematic assessment of their homeless learners (Comprehensive Adult Student Assessment System, 1991). The primary purpose of assessment in this case was to determine readiness for vocational training. The Employability Competency System Appraisal was administered to learners in an effort to measure their basic skills in a functional context. The California State Department of Education contracted with the Comprehensive Adult Student Assessment System (CASAS) to administer the tests. The homeless agencies involved were located in several areas across the state and were operated by a variety of public and nonprofit organizations.

CASAS has classified four functioning levels which are identified by a range of scores. A score below 200 indicates that learners will "have difficulty with the basic literacy and computational skills necessary to function in employment and in the community" (Comprehensive Adult Student Assessment System, 1991, p. 11). According to CASAS, adults scoring in this range would have difficulty writing, handling paychecks, computing wages, and following simple written directions and safety procedures. On the reading portion of the assessment, 3.9% of the participants scored in this range, and 12.8% scored in this range in the math assessment (Comprehensive Adult Student Assessment System, 1991).

The next functional level, indicated by scores between 200 and 214, places learners at a level where they would "have difficulty pursuing other than entry level programs requiring minimal literacy skills. . . . At this level, adults can function in entry level jobs that involve oral communication but in which most required tasks are demonstrated" (Comprehensive Adult Student Assessment System, 1991, p. 11). On the reading assessment, 14.6% of the learners scored at this level, and 28.7% scored at this level in math. In other words, 18.5% of the learners could benefit from basic skills remediation in reading and 41.5% of them could benefit from math instruction. Only 13.6% of the learners indicated that Spanish was their native language (Comprehensive Adult Student Assessment System, 1991).

Ropers (1988) and Hagen (1987) indicate surprise that so many shelter residents are high school graduates. Literacy educators know, however, that the possession of high school credentials does not always correlate with high or proficient reading levels. It is interesting to note that the previous CASAS report (1990) on California programs indicated nearly 16% of the learners scored at the lowest functioning level on reading tests. This discrepancy is not clearly explained and most likely is an indicator of how difficult such measurements are to obtain. While acknowledging measurement limitations, it is clear that many homeless adults can benefit from an opportunity to improve their basic skills.

PROVIDING PREPARATION THAT LEADS TO THE ACQUISITION OF CREDENTIALS

In our society, many training opportunities and jobs are closed to people who do not have at least a high school equivalency certificate. More than ever, report Berlin and Sum (1988), the labor market distinguishes between those with a high school diploma and those who left school before graduation. Dail (1990) noted in her study that 50% of the women heading homeless families reported not having graduated from high school. In the California CASAS report, with an *n* of 3,271 subjects, 49.4% of the learners had not completed more than eleven years of school (Comprehensive Adult Student Assessment System, 1991). Ropers (1988), when comparing data from seven cities and two states, found the percentage of non-high school graduates in the homeless populations studied ranging from 36 to 69%. In a study comparing mothers from housed families with those requesting shelter, Shinn, Knickman, and Weitzman (1991) found approximately 60% of both samples to have less than a high school education.

Literacy education programs for the homeless can provide at least a starting place for those residents who would like to prepare for the General Education Development (GED) test. The barriers inherent with homeless environments make it difficult to offer sustained preparation in the manner of more traditional settings. The testing process itself is enmeshed in paperwork requirements. The need for transportation to and from testing sites adds to the difficulty. Also, getting test results can be a lengthy process, and homeless adults typically do not stay in one location very long.

Nevertheless, for many homeless adults, the shelter stay represents an opportunity to pursue something that may have only been a dream in the past. In some instances, simply delving into practice tests shows the learner the GED is obtainable. Once acquired, it can never be taken away and offers, at the very least, an entry point to additional training previously closed to the learner.

ENHANCING THE LIFESKILLS OF HOMELESS ADULT LEARNERS

Literacy educators have long embraced the concept of teaching basic skills through the use of immediately relevant materials, although few have studied and reported on the actual processes involved (Fingeret, 1990). Educators quickly began developing curriculum materials that reflected the immediate needs of homeless learners, if for no other reason than to feel relevant to their learner's lives. One of the first lifeskills curriculum efforts included learning modules in several lifeskill areas: getting a job, finding a place to live, managing a budget, getting organized, managing child-care, and getting proper identification (Stuart, 1990). The modules were developed as shelter residents asked for assistance.

A state-by-state review of the Stewart B. McKinney funded

educational initiatives revealed 28 educational techniques or approaches other than traditional basic skills remediation or GED preparation (U.S. Department of Education, 1989). Examples included life coping skills, personal growth, independent living skills, parenting, and self-help skills. Topics related to employment were the most represented areas, followed by money management and personal growth. In at least one location a lifeskills curriculum was developed using an alcohol abuse recovery program as its content. The materials developed in both of these lifeskills projects have been primarily learner-centered, in that the learners themselves expressed needs for particular subject areas.

Homeless adults in shelters, in soup kitchens, on the streets, and in other locations have uppermost in their minds immediate, crucial basic needs such as food, housing, clothing, health care, child care, and transportation. If literacy instruction is to be successfully offered in many homeless situations, it must present reasonable, concrete strategies for these needs while addressing broader goals such as communication and coping skills. Lifeskills programs are not a substitute for traditional math, reading, and writing instruction. Correctly developed, however, lifeskills units incorporate basic literacy skills into a format that helps learners address their most pressing needs.

The lifeskills approach itself plays a role in the invitation-to-learn process initiated by instructors. Quite often, a foray into a lifeskills unit leads to an expressed interest in the GED or other more basic literacy assistance. In this manner, the lifeskills units act as a gateway or path to other interests or topics. Sometimes, the lifeskills curriculum can ease the problems of anxiety or distrust by introducing material that is not associated with past unsuccessful learning experiences. The lifeskills units represent several options to learners. They can select an area of study themselves, work independently or with a group, and complete objectives in a short period of time—even in one evening.

Literacy educators have found the lifeskills approach to be a valuable asset in gaining access to homeless shelters or transitional programs. While many shelter providers have no idea how basic skills remediation would fit into their overall program, they almost always see the possibilities with lifeskills approaches. One of the most exciting parts of the lifeskills role for literacy education is that it is always evolving and growing. The possibilities would only be limited by the immediate needs of the shelter residents.

ASSISTING IN TRANSACTIONAL ACTIVITIES REQUIRING BASIC LITERACY SKILLS AND READING COMPREHENSION

One way that people engage in literacy activities is to complete forms, tax returns, job applications, and other paperwork. An inability to cope with such tasks may be the result of low basic skills, excessively difficult forms, a lack of practice, a lack of opportunity to focus on the task, or a combination of all these factors. Yet many homeless adults have an immediate need to complete such forms. Hollingsworth et al. (1990) refer to the secondary needs of homeless adults as those arising once a person has activated the social service system "and is seeking to make it work for them. Literacy problems impede communication. Standardized forms and letters must be acted upon in a timely manner" (p. 2). Hollingsworth et al. note that the social service system "requires of the client high levels of ability both to comprehend and act on complex demands related to documentation" (p. 8).

Literacy educators can take part in this process by offering one-on-one or group assistance and by explaining what documents mean. In pure survival terms, this may be the most important function the educator can perform. Hollingsworth et al. see literacy instructors as planting seeds for the future. "Many homeless persons look at the goal of continuing their education as a long-term prospect for the future. Although they do recognize the extra hours in the shelter are well-spent working toward that goal, others stay focused on their immediate needs revolving around jobs and places to live" (p. 14). Teachers may have contact with learners that they never would have had by helping out with transactional literacy tasks.

PROVIDING A SPECIALLY TAILORED EDUCATION COMPONENT TO EXISTING SHELTER PROGRAMS

Many shelter directors and service providers to the homeless express the value of education but are unable to provide it to their residents. With families sleeping in cars just outside their doors while waiting for a room, some providers simply cannot include basic skills education, GED training, or lifeskills education in their mix of services. In many instances, they do not know how nor do they have adequate staff. Literacy education programs can accomplish what the providers cannot accomplish. Efforts range from placing an instructor on site to handle learner requests as homeless adults come into the shelter to operating an educational program at another location. In the latter case, by providing transportation and child care, residents at several locations can attend to educational needs without placing an extra burden on shelter providers.

Educational programs can be tailored to meet specifically identified needs of residents as a part of the shelter program. For instance, one literacy program offered a weekly lifeskills session to all the residents at a shelter for battered women. By designing a cooperative arrangement, the literacy program was able to reach a particular segment of the homeless population while the shelter providers were able to add a significant component to their ongoing program. One program in North Carolina operates at a local church. A bus goes to several area shelters and brings homeless adults to the church where they participate in lifeskills and literacy training. Child care is provided. For some of the shelter providers, the one-night-a-week program affords them their only opportunity to provide at least some educational opportunities to their residents.

PROVIDING A LINK BETWEEN LEARNERS
AND THEIR COMMUNITY

It would not be much of a stretch of the imagination to describe some homeless project literacy instructors as living, breathing resource centers. Instructors working in the shelters soon become repositories of information about services and activities available in the community. In some instances, community-based resource guides developed specifically for this purpose have been incorporated into lifeskills activities (Stuart, 1990). The instructor becomes a link between the learner and the city, available services, and educational opportunities. Goodman, Saxe, and Harvey (1991) admonish shelter providers to promote as many connections as possible among homeless adults themselves and between homeless adults and their communities. Such efforts might ameliorate the psychological trauma of homelessness.

One connective role that literacy education plays is to serve as the literacy program's link to the community and related social service agencies. Developing a project that serves homeless adults certainly puts the community in the community college, so to speak. Program developers and instructors can quickly become enmeshed in the array of services and organizations that surround homeless needs. They may participate in working groups, coalitions, and workshops. They may also become referring agents and partners.

SERVING AS AN ANCHOR FOR
OTHER PROGRAMS

Adult basic education sponsored literacy programs have long been criticized for their oppressive rules, inflexibility, and bureaucracies (Fingeret, 1985). Ironically, these characteristics can become strengths when a strong, secure presence is needed to stimulate program development. For example, a local church may desire to serve the homeless but does not know how to get started. They may choose to team up with an ABE program in order to accomplish greater goals. The literacy program administrators develop a schedule and hire an instructor. Perhaps the joint project may center on the lifeskills approach, with the intent to invite homeless adults to participate. As the program develops, the church and other involved organizations can begin offering a variety of services and programs and developing a strong outreach effort. Rather than standing on its own, the literacy program in this example is just one part of a more comprehensive effort.

PROVIDING HOMELESS ADULTS WITH
A LINK TO THEMSELVES

Literacy instructors across the nation are famous for their love of success stories such as those about the GED graduate who overcame tremendous odds. They tell stories of attitude changes, improvements in self-esteem, and personal discoveries and public victories. These educators have been taken to task for their stories which are considered by some to distract from the real work of literacy education, teaching reading (Fox, 1986). But the stories do indicate positive movement. Literacy educators working with homeless adults also thrive on the stories as they cope with the traumatic environment of homelessness.

One instructor in North Carolina commented to her supervisor that an incident the night before in the emergency shelter made her feel very positive about her efforts. The learner, she said, was quite reluctant to pursue any educational activities, even though she had indicated to the instructor that she had difficulties reading. The instructor coaxed her into listening to a beginning level, instructional reading tape. Still seemingly anxious and reluctant, the learner sat off by herself with headphones, tape recorder, and workbook. After a few minutes, reported the instructor, her face broke into a huge, brilliant smile! "She realized she understood what she was hearing and that she could do the work. She *could* learn!" the instructor said.

In hundreds of shelters, soup kitchens, and other related sites, instructors are making connections with people who are enduring crisis-oriented circumstances. Compounding the problems of homelessness for women, for instance, are the high incidences of physical, sexual, and emotional abuse which are often suffered just prior to requesting shelter (Goodman, Saxe, & Harvey, 1991). In the midst of trauma, the literacy educator provides opportunities for homeless adults to interact with a caring person and to interact with themselves. Considering that literacy educators have historically received high marks from learners for their concern, genuineness, and respect (Fingeret, 1985), it is little surprise the same characteristics are manifesting themselves in educators working with homeless adults.

The opportunities for learners to make connections with themselves comes in many forms. An instructor kept requesting math worksheets for her learners at an emergency shelter. When asked why she used so many of the worksheets, she replied, "Because people keep asking me if they can try some math problems. Some of them have said they aren't sure they can think or do such work anymore. They want to know they can still function mentally." Other learners may simply ask to borrow a book and sit with other students. "I don't do this anymore," said one homeless adult. "I need to try out my mind."

These outcomes are not even implicit in the McKinney Act definitions of basic skills remediation and literacy training. Such interactions may not be reported to education departments as success indicators. Historically, literacy educators have always provided such opportunities to learners. Because of the tremendous attrition rates in literacy classes (Hunter & Harman, 1979), such successes were often the only ones manifest. In homeless shelters, attrition is a given. Educators are capitalizing on their unique capacity to offer a little success in the midst of discouragement.

DISCUSSION

Several roles for literacy education programs for homeless adults have evolved since the state literacy initiatives began. The variety of these roles illustrates how difficult it can be to define literacy in the context of homelessness. The National Literacy Act of 1991 (PL 102-73) includes a definition of literacy that provides a useful framework. It is defined as

> an individual's ability to read, write, and speak in English, and compute and solve problems at levels of proficiencies necessary to function on the job and in society, to achieve one's goals, and develop one's knowledge and potential.

Literacy education for homeless adults provides them opportunities to further use and develop their abilities to meet their own needs. It ranges from serving the nonreader to preparing the GED candidate and from assisting the learner with transactions that require literacy skills to teaching basic skills in the context of lifeskills materials. Literacy education for the homeless incorporates a variety of instruction activities that are purposeful. "People read, write, talk, and think about real ideas and information . . . " (Langer, 1986, p. 7).

The authors take a view of literacy that has learners acquiring more tools of communication and more strategies for solving their immediate problems. Reading levels and functional literacy levels are useful concepts for instructional design but are not to be used as a sorting mechanism for who will be served by the literacy program. Taking Langer's (1986) view that "literacy is an activity, a way of thinking, not a set of skills . . . " (p. 7), the authors propose that many more homeless adults than those scoring below an arbitrarily designated reading or functional level can benefit from literacy education.

Homeless adults are also adult learners with immediate, personally defined needs for instruction. The next chapter will consider the homeless adult learners and ramifications for literacy programs.

CHAPTER 3

The Homeless Adult Learner

As has been illustrated in previous chapters, developing and implementing literacy programs for homeless adults is considerably more complex than simply transporting current practices into homeless shelters or related locations. The barriers to education are imposing, beginning with difficult learning environments and shortages of instructional time. Several roles for literacy education for homeless adults have emerged, however, and the energy for the challenge appears to remain high.

The keys to successful programs include program design flexibility, innovative approaches to instruction, and appropriate educational facilitators. Perhaps the key that will have the greatest impact, however, involves the understanding of the adult learner. A basic knowledge of the adult learner by both program designers and instructors will ensure an appropriate foundation and enhance educational efforts where "facilitators and learners are full partners in the learning experience" (Galbraith, 1991, p. 2). This chapter will examine adult learner characteristics and will consider the effect of homelessness on these characteristics.

Program designers charged with developing effective programs for literacy education for homeless adults must recognize and address adult learning needs. These needs do not become irrelevant or disappear when a person becomes a member of an unhoused population. If anything, the learning needs become even more important to understand. Adult learners have the need for respect, safety, recognition of personal experience, inclusion in the learning process, immediate application of skills, and availability for learning. These needs will be discussed.

RESPECT

Vella (1989), describing respect, says that "the learners must feel honored, respected as a person, not for what he or she knows but for themselves" (p. 22). Adult learners, adds Knowles (1970), "have a need to be treated with respect, to make their own decisions, to be seen as unique human beings" (p. 40). Knowles continues, "learners tend to avoid, resist, and resent situations in which they are treated like children—being told what to do, embarrassed, punished, judged" (p. 40).

Those homeless adults with a need for improved basic skills may labor under the double stigma of homelessness and being under-educated, making the principle of respect even more meaningful. Russell (1988) reflects upon the shame that homeless women in Baltimore felt because of the loss of their homes and, in most instances, their children. They often reacted to their shame by seeking to "pass" for their housed counterparts by wearing certain clothing or carrying certain packages in public. Beder (1991) also describes adults trying to pass for literate. Discussing the stigma of illiteracy in this society, Beder writes that low-literate adults "are perceived to be dependent and incapable of succeeding without the intervention of experts, who, with good intentions, are charged with 'making them over' " (p. 76).

Fingeret (1990) notes that "learners must be viewed as capable of meaningful participation. This is often difficult because we have inherited a deficit perspective in which the skills, world view, and attitudes of adults with low print literacy abilities have been dismissed or downgraded" (p. 40). The principle of respect takes on added significance when working with adults already struggling for recognition regardless of their literacy skill levels.

How is respect manifested in literacy programs for homeless adults? It begins at the outset. The public often exhibits a differential concern for various groups of homeless people, with women and children generally getting more sympathy than unemployed men (Dluhy, 1990). Adopting an attitude of respect that applies to all homeless learners regardless of their particular circumstances and problems is a challenge for program planners and instructors. Homeless people who have overwhelming problems and little chance of exiting homelessness or poverty should not be written off as uneducable.

A review of the literature about homelessness in this country reveals that considerable attention has been focused on the subgroups of the homeless. These subgroups include the mentally ill, those who abuse substances and alcohol, and poor women with children (Ropers, 1988). The danger in this labeling process is in the manifestation of a system that seeks out those deemed most likely to benefit from literacy training and ignores the others.

Adult educators working with homeless adults would be disrespectful of the high levels of creativity and ingenuity, for instance, of many homeless people (Koegel, Burnam, & Farr, 1990) who are typically excluded from programs because of their deficiencies. Coles (1987) refers to an educator's view of a person that acknowledges "a person who is intelligent, who is capable of learning, who has enormous potential, who cannot be written off with various categories and labels, who can be transformed" (p. 482). Examining and letting go of preconceived notions about homeless people is the beginning of respect.

Perhaps the most significant action that shows respect for learners is to ask them what they want. According to Kazemek (1984), educator John Dewey believed that "one can find out more about people and their interests, needs, beliefs, and values by asking them, by talking things over with them, by asking them 'where the shoe pinches' " (p. 65). The educator, adds Kazemek, cannot make assumptions about what people feel and need. Russell (1988) notes how the women she studied in Baltimore's homeless population were rarely if ever asked what they needed. They were not included in the design of programs meant to serve them either.

Respecting homeless adult learners involves asking them what their educational needs are and designing curriculum materials and approaches that reflect these needs. This can be a tall order when shelter operators often have strong feelings about what specific skills should be taught to their residents. This is especially true when skills selected by shelter staff are not seen as important by their clients. Galbraith (1991) refers to learners' felt or prescribed needs, the former reflecting the wants, desires, and wishes of the learners, and the latter referring to the knowledge, skills, and attitudes facilitators desire for learners. The tension between felt and prescribed needs is particularly acute in literacy programs for the homeless. It often relates to what shelter providers want for their residents rather than what the educators want.

For example, a director of a family emergency shelter may believe what the learners need is a basic course in managing their lives, including budgeting and jobs. The underlying assumption is a common belief that inability to cope and take charge of one's life is a root cause of homelessness. The learners, on the other hand, when given a choice, may prefer to read through GED practice questions or complete a self-esteem lifeskills unit. Giving choices in some small way gives some measure of control back to adults who have experienced little control during their homeless status (Rivlin & Imbimbo, 1989). The choices of food, entry into a shelter, shower, and bedtimes are severely limited in many shelter situations. Asking learners what they want represents the return of at least a modicum of control.

SAFETY

The principle of safety for adult learners involves two aspects of program design: physical and emotional safety. An intimidated or threatened person is unlikely to benefit from any educational program no matter how timely, relevant, and respectful. Goodman, Saxe, and Harvey (1991) write that shelter staff "should ensure that the shelter environment is physically safe and secure, because violence, substance abuse, and other disturbances in the shelter may inhibit occupants from establishing or maintaining social connections" (p. 1223). The authors were concerned for the physical and psychological well-being of homeless people, but the significance for learning environments is apparent as well. An example of a physical safety issue that sabotaged an otherwise sensible program idea was related by an instructor in the southeast United States.

Two shelters were located within a hundred yards of each other. All that stood between them was a tiny chapel belonging to one shelter and a parking area belonging to the second. The literacy project coordinator decided it was prudent to offer nightly instruction at just one of the sites while extending an invitation to residents of the nearby shelter to join the learning activities. Referral forms were developed, help at both sites was enlisted, and instructors waited for the neighbors to join the class. That never happened! No one crossed the parking area. Why? Because the parking area had become the designated pickup point for the homeless adults going to the city overflow shelter. The area was perceived as highly dangerous, even to the homeless residents of the two adjacent shelters. Potential students preferred no instruction at all to making the brief trek next door.

Emotional safety involves the learners' beliefs that they can participate in an educational program without ridicule or embarrassment. Fingeret and Danin (1991) make a distinction between private and public use of literacy skills. "Private situations occur when a student is alone or with well-known and trusted others, such as in their tutoring groups or with their families at home. Public situations occur when other people are involved who are not known or trusted, or when skills use is opened up to the scrutiny of such persons" (p. 14). They note that students develop and use their literacy skills both "inside" and "outside" the program. "Inside the program is a haven for many students, a place where there is potential to feel valued rather than devalued, central rather than marginalized, part of a team rather than isolated" (p. 13).

The literacy program taking place either inside a homeless shelter or at an alternative location may allow little private use of new skills since the situation may not feel private at all. The students in Fingeret and Danin's (1991) study spoke of their concerns about conducting themselves "properly in public situations" (p. 14). If the shelter environment feels unsafe or public in the first place, participation may be very short term or nonexistent for basic skills learners.

If instruction is to take place inside homeless shelters, great care must be taken to secure a safe teaching environment. Some shelters, particularly the emergency or overflow types, may have looser rules about who can enter the shelter and in what condition. Teaching in these circumstances may be counterproductive. Some female residents may feel physically unsafe in the presence of men and will not participate in programs that are coeducational. Program designers will have to factor in physical safety and consider alternatives such as establishing women-only groups or transporting shelter guests to a different learning environment.

Designing for emotional safety partly involves privacy. The instructional area should not be amidst the major traffic flow in the shelter. Ensuring privacy in shelter settings, however, is difficult, if not impossible. In some instances in the past, shelter operators have offered learning space they considered to be private, relative to the overall shelter atmosphere. Instructors found cause to lament the lack of privacy.

> The little room that the teacher had been using for instruction was given to the new college social work intern. The instructor was moved to the shelter television room. For several weeks, she used the top of the television as a desk, and had to situate herself and her students around other residents and sometimes their children. The residents would often lie down on the couch to watch television. Doing her best in such a difficult situation, the instructor soon realized that people were no longer coming for instruction. She concluded that the lack of privacy made many women reluctant to participate.

Program designers have to consider the shelter environment, work with shelter providers who place high premium on any available space, and consider learners' needs for safety.

EXPERIENCE

The principle of experience involves valuing the experience of the learner, recognizing experience as strength, and building educational activities upon the foundation of that experience. Vella (1989) teaches that "learners learn best when what they are learning is directly related to their own life experiences" (p. 22). Adult learners are very aware when instructional efforts and materials bear no relationship to their personal experience.

Knowles (1970) says that "an adult is what he has done" (p. 44). Knowles further elaborates that "to an adult, his experience is him. He defines who he is, establishes his self-identity, in terms of his accumulation of a unique set of experiences" (p. 44). If these experiences are not recognized and incorporated into the learning environment, the learner may feel rejected as a person. This learning principle is acutely important when working with homeless adults already struggling for recognition.

Because of their experience base, adult learners have much to contribute to the learning of others. Knowles thinks of adult learners as valuable resources in and of themselves. They also have a broad base of experience upon which to acquire and understand new information and knowledge. Fingeret (1991) notes the value of the experience principle when designing curriculum. "It appears that we learn by relating new information to what we already know—we make sense out of text by relating it to our existing cognitive structures. The implication is that students will learn most efficiently when the instructional materials respect and incorporate students' prior experiences, culture, and aspirations, as well as the contexts within which literacy skills will be used" (p. 8).

An example of not incorporating the experience principle is illustrated by the experience of a paraprofessional nutrition aide who arrived at a family shelter to teach caregivers of children food safety principles. "When you are in your kitchen," she said, "always be conscious of how long certain foods can go without refrigeration. You wouldn't want your children or yourself to become ill!" The instructor, already working under frustrating conditions with many interruptions and inadequate child care provisions, was determined to stick to her curriculum and provide this important information. Only later did she realize that her clients did not *have* a kitchen of their own, and perhaps had never actually had one. What she was teaching was not in their immediate experience.

INCLUSION IN THE LEARNING PROCESS

The adult learning principle of inclusion requires educators to design programs that avoid leaving people out and focus on bringing people in. The new program director at a large mission that serves men with alcohol abuse problems noted the difference in current versus previous program efforts. "Before, we had so many ways to keep people out. Now we focus on all the ways we can keep people in. We invite them in as many ways as possible to stay with us, rather than directing so much energy towards infractions that result in departure." The principle of inclusion can be thought of an an invitation to join, to learn, and to stay.

An inclusive program issues invitations by design. Strategies for designing inclusive programs include providing transportation so that those who could otherwise not attend are brought into the learning process. Providing child care allows more people to be included, as does offering individual tutor/volunteer support if a particular student needs it. Shelter operators can make meals available at alternate times for those residents who would like to be involved in instruction but cannot miss their meals. Providing an array of instructional options invites more people to participate in learning.

One evening, a resident of a semi-transitional shelter housing 25 men and 10 women kept interrupting the instructor with questions. He was not enrolled in the literacy program at the shelter. When the man asked the instructor to look up something for him in the phone book, she good naturedly gave him directions as to where the phone book was located. "That won't do me any good," he protested. "I'll just get mixed up when I look at it and not know what it says." The instructor then told him others were at that very moment learning how to read, and he could join them. "No way," he insisted. "I don't want them to know."

Thinking inclusively, the instructor invited the resident to listen to an audiocassette math program and brush up on his math skills. According to the instructor, "He was delighted when he put on the head phones and realized he could do the work *without* others knowing anything about his reading problems! Most people seem to feel okay about refreshing their math skills. He certainly did. For those few hours, he was included in the learning rather than being left out. His joy was obvious!"

IMMEDIATE APPLICATION OF SKILLS

Perhaps the adult learning principle of immediacy is the one most adhered to by literacy program providers serving the homeless as much from necessity as from a knowledge of adult learning. Vella (1989) notes that "learners must see how they can use their new knowledge, skills, and attitudes immediately" (p. 22). Adults enter educational activities in a problem-centered frame of mind, writes Knowles (1970). "They engage in learning largely in response to pressures they feel from their current life situation. To adults, education is a process of improving their ability to deal with life problems they face now" (p. 48). When viewed through the immediacy principle, educators of homeless adults may have more opportunity to affect change in people's lives then do literacy instructors in more traditional environments. They are able to follow Sticht's (1987) advice and teach basic skills in the context of immediately useful information.

Kazemek (1985), writing about different kinds of literacy skills, refers to transactional discourse where "the individual uses language as a means or a tool to do something" (p. 334). Residents of shelters almost universally have immediate need for literacy skills, particularly transactional literacy skills. For instance, a VISTA volunteer, in her report to the City of Raleigh Human Resources Department, expressed concern about the amount of paperwork required by city and county agencies and the difficulties many homeless people have completing it (Hollingsworth et al., 1990, p. 7). While the author viewed literacy education as generally a secondary need of homeless adults, it certainly becomes a primary need when transactions must be made in a timely manner.

Immediate learning needs of homeless adults, while often of a transactional nature, such as filling out tax forms and job applications, extend to other areas as well. Many adults are seeking their GED credentials and choose to use shelter time as an opportunity to work towards that goal. Some homeless adults are struggling to meet the needs of their children and desire to help with homework but lack skills. Unfortunately, many high school graduates read at below high school levels, and use the instructional opportunity to improve their reading.

Kazemek's (1985) poetic and expressive discourse can be represented in shelters as well. Helen M., a resident at a semi-transitional shelter, was also a poet. Her literacy skills for transactions were high, but she desired help with her writing. Through her association with shelter staff and the literacy instructor, she was interviewed by the local newspaper. Both her poems and her picture were featured in a front page article. The instructor helped her practice for her interview and edit the poems she was submitting. Literacy as communication was demonstrated in this situation, as was the principle of immediacy.

The immediacy principle is reflected in the lifeskills curriculum efforts that have been a result of several homeless literacy projects. Stunned by the immediate or yesterday needs of homeless adults, instructors in many areas of the country began developing instructional units to go along with the those urgent needs. The result has been teaching modules on getting a job, finding a place to live, working with social service agencies, helping children in school, managing money, getting organized, coping with legal issues, and dozens of other topics. Reflecting the city-by-city, area-by-area differences, these lifeskills units have typically been "homemade" and tailored to specific locations. They reflect the principle of immediacy and the learners' needs for immediate knowledge.

The "Lifeskills for the Homeless" material developed in North Carolina (Stuart, 1990) was the result of daily instructional work at a large family shelter. Armed with traditional literacy materials (e.g. GED books, reading programs, and math practice sheets) the author soon discovered that residents had more immediate needs. These were sometimes as specific as knowing literally how to use the phone and communicate with the answering party. Much to the surprise of the instructor, her homemade "telephone call sheet" was quickly being carted around by shelter residents and actually used.

It is possible that some homeless women with children are actually starting from ground zero towards their independence (Walsh, 1990). Dail (1990), in her study of homeless mothers, observed that "many of the mothers have never established themselves as functional, self-sufficient, autonomous adults, due in part to having been socialized in a cycle of poverty themselves. Most have long histories of interpersonal and economic problems as well as distinct patterns of residential instability" (p. 294). These adults have immediate needs at a survival level.

AVAILABILITY FOR LEARNING

Harman (1987) explains his "availability for learning theory." "Being available for learning implies readiness to change in some aspect of one's life" (p. 71). According to Harman, the learner will become available to literacy instruction only "when he or she perceives the need to develop literacy skills because they have become a part of a goal that person wishes to attain" (p. 71). A favorable response to literacy instruction, says Harman, is not likely if it is not perceived as necessary. As important as the method of instruction is, notes Harman, it is "the availability of people for learning that will ultimately determine whether or not instruction will be effective" (p. 71).

Effective instructors will have to find out in what areas learners are available. The availability principle is especially pertinent when working with homeless adults and should lead to some very effective instruction because there are so many immediate needs. A shelter resident who has one week to find an apartment is most likely available to learn how to read and decode classified ads. Likewise, a homeless adult who is attempting to complete the application process for disability payments is available to learn the language of the application and the literacy tasks necessary to complete it.

DISCUSSION

The world of the homeless adult learner is set in a precarious environment, and this carries consequences for the established principles of adult development and education. The shelter resident is first and foremost an adult learner. It would be easy to view homeless adults as victims or personally at fault for their current circumstances. Their need for respect, safety, inclusion, immediacy, and availability to learn may be neglected in favor of providing preselected curriculum materials based on socially-assigned objectives. Homeless adult learners, however, have the same needs as any other adult learner. The challenge to instructors is to recognize and meet these needs in the context of the crisis and emotional trauma that homelessness causes (Goodman, Saxe, & Harvey, 1991).

Potential instructors must be willing to examine not only their teaching style and methods but also their accepted beliefs about poverty and social justice. The program designer is faced with the task of developing a training plan to orient instructors and to aid them in ceasing to perpetuate myths and unconscious victim blaming attitudes that permeate society (Pardek, 1990; Ryan, 1971). Teacher training is every bit as crucial in regard to program design as it is in fitting traditional literacy practices to homeless adults in shelters. In chapter four, the principles and necessary factors in teacher selection and training will be discussed.

CHAPTER 4

Instructor Selection and Training

Teacher behaviors take on additional significance when the educational arena is related to homelessness. Knowles (1970) believes that "the behavior of the teacher probably influences the character of the learning climate more than any other single factor" (p. 4). In this chapter, desirable instructor behaviors will be reviewed as they relate to working with homeless adults. These behaviors include showing respect for homeless adults, being able to relate to the learners, possessing instructional and assessment knowledge, tolerating constant change, knowing how to communicate with shelter providers, understanding community resources, and maintaining accountability procedures related to the sponsoring education organization.

SHOWING RESPECT

Knowles (1970) writes that "the teacher conveys in many ways whether his attitude is one of interest and respect for the students or whether he sees them essentially as receiving sets for his transmission of wisdom" (p. 38). This show of respect can be difficult when instructors follow the public's lead in forming opinions about homelessness (Pardek, 1990). As noted earlier, the public often exhibits a differential concern for various groups of homeless people, with women and children generally getting more sympathy than unemployed men (Dluhy, 1990). Project instructors may have internalized these same feelings.

Alcohol and other substance abuse is prevalent among certain homeless populations (Sosin & Grossman, 1991). Illegal resident status is commonplace among non-English speaking homeless people. Instances of child abuse and neglect surface frequently at shelters (Milburn & D'Ercole, 1991). Showing respect for the learner is not always easy when instructors have personal views that conflict with some behavior they are witnessing.

Other educators have discussed variations on conveying respect that have particular applications here. Fingeret (1989), in discussing participatory learning practices for nonreader education, speaks of learner dignity and diversity. Nonreaders, she notes, are "the creators of their own social lives, as imperfect as those lives may appear by middle-class standards" (p. 9). Nonreading adults are diverse and multitalented and, most often, function quite well in their social environments. Both the dignity and diversity of homeless adults, regardless of their current circumstances and reading ability, must be respected. This can be a challenge!

> The women from several shelters were seated around the tables at the once-a-week literacy/lifeskills program for homeless adults. Linda M. did not want to be there and loudly refused to sign the enrollment forms for the sponsoring education agency. "I hate this. I didn't want to come. They made me come anyway, and I won't sign anything!" The project director was upset. The literacy instructor, however, spoke with Linda. "I don't blame you. You're right. You didn't want to come tonight. I might not have either." The result was a rapid lessening in tension and the inclusion of Linda without the paperwork. The next week she willingly completed the documents.

RELATING TO THE LEARNERS

Fellenz et al. (1981), in a study of one state's literacy program outcomes, found that "the teacher trait most important for individual growth and development was the ability to relate to the students" (p. 29). Galbraith (1991) reviews characteristics that can help educators be more effective in facilitating adult learning. These include being more concerned about the learners than about things and events, and being warm, loving, caring, and accepting of learners.

If a prerequisite to relating to learners is having to have had the same experiences, teacher selection would be quite difficult. In some instances, though, instructors for homeless literacy projects have been homeless themselves, or more likely have worked with homeless adults in other situations. Relating also means tapping into similarities rather than differences. The human condition and range of emotions is universal and encompasses everyone. In these terms instructors can demonstrate their relationship to their learners.

An understanding of basic human needs as illustrated by Maslow (1971) allows instructors to demonstrate their ability to relate to homeless learners. An instructor working in a family shelter found that she was able to relate to the women because she had once received subsistence payments and foodstamps, although she had never been homeless. In another instance, an instructor related to a woman who refused to leave her child at the child care center before coming to the literacy program.

> All of the other women left their children but not Myra. As a result, the instructor had to contend with two preschoolers crawling all over the classroom and all over her. The instructor could tell the mother was distracted, and so was everyone else. At first, the instructor was upset because the presence of the children made conducting the program so difficult. But, then she realized how reluctant she would be to leave her two children with people she didn't know while already living in a shelter full of people she didn't know. She understood how threatening it might be to have to rely totally on other people's good intentions.

This instructor was able to relate to the learner because she recognized common experiences. Marlowe, Branson, Childress, and Parker (1991) refer to these relational skills as interpersonal communication skills. Included in their compilation of teacher competencies are awareness of social and cultural backgrounds, an understanding of psychological and physical problems, an accepting, openminded attitude, and a knowledge of gender and ethnic discrimination. These competencies were established for literacy instructors working with the general population, but certainly carry over to instructors working with homeless persons.

DEMONSTRATING APPROPRIATE INSTRUCTIONAL AND ASSESSMENT PRACTICES

Weber (1975), in her review of issues in adult literacy, is alarmed to note what she considers to be an undue emphasis on relying on instructor respect for students and ability to relate to them. "The professional quality that a teacher might bring to adult classes . . . tend to be less valued . . . than the ability to get along well with students, to recognize their dignity as human beings, and to provide positive support for their awkward attempts to become fluent readers" (p. 160). While valuing the aforementioned qualities, Weber expresses concern that literacy instructors' knowledge base might be lacking. Fingeret (1985) notes that relating well to learners "will serve no purpose if one is unable to help students progress as quickly as possible" (p. 176). While the instructor in a homeless literacy project may very well be serving a purpose regardless of instructional success, a thorough grounding in reading, writing, and math instruction is required, and particularly in programs for homeless adults.

Camperell, Rachal, and Pierce (1983), studied the characteristics and training needs of literacy instructors in Mississippi. They found that while nearly three-fourths of that state's literacy students likely required extensive reading instruction, only 26% of the surveyed instructors had received any formal training in teaching reading. The instructors comfortably viewed themselves as resource persons in their classrooms and relied on prepackaged instructional material for reading instruction. Instructors in literacy programs for homeless adults frequently come from some pool of instructors serving the broader literacy effort and may need more specific instructional training.

Instructors working with homeless adults are called upon to meet the expressed needs of their learners—needs that typically run the gamut from beginning reading to algebra and geometry. It is unrealistic to expect such a range of skills from an instructor, particularly as they pertain to teaching nonreaders. However, instructors should be selected in part for their demonstrated competency in a variety of subject matters.

Marlowe and others (1991) identify four broad teacher competency areas needed by literacy instructors. These include (a) establishing and sustaining interpersonal communication relationships with adult learners; (b) effectively assessing and diagnosing learner's strengths and weaknesses: (c) selecting methodologies and materials for individual learners and groups of learners; and (d) participating in meaningful program evaluation (p. 156). Instructors working with homeless adults should demonstrate strengths in each of these areas, relative to the literacy program role they are filling in their particular situation.

CAPACITY FOR TOLERATING CHANGE

If there is a certainty while providing literacy education programs to homeless adults, it is change. The instructional environments can change as quickly as overnight. Rapid turnover in shelter populations and daily fluctuation in attendance at shelters and soup kitchens are the norm. Turnover in shelter staff is frequent and can alter the instructional environment and learner participation immediately.

Learners themselves change during one day. An instructor working with Spanish-speaking homeless men in the morning found she could not work with the same men at night at an emergency shelter because they were either exhausted or under the influence of alcohol. Learners who are mentally ill can change within an instructional hour.

> Mary G. had been working with her instructor for about an hour, practicing writing some sentences that had been giving her trouble. People were coming in to use the phone in the dining room, which was a common occurrence. On this particular evening, though, Mary began to get agitated. "I think I want to make a

call now," she said, and got up to stand by the phone. As the caller persisted in his conversation, Mary became increasingly upset and started making hissing sounds. The instructor in effect closed up shop.

A subtle shift in operating policies of a shelter can completely alter the current literacy program for the better or for the worse. After a staffing change at a local emergency shelter, the evening instructor was no longer allowed to go upstairs and tell people personally he was available for instruction. He had to rely on an announcement being made by the new night monitor. Attendance plummeted.

Instructors must exhibit a tolerance for change and a flexibility that carries them through the constantly altering landscape of homelessness and surrounding services. In a shelter in one southern city, dinner is served every night of the week by volunteers from various organizations. The food is brought in and usually served around 7:00 p.m. The instructor reported to his supervisor one morning that he was upset and depressed about the previous evening. "I wasn't able to teach for even one minute. Whoever was bringing dinner didn't show, and it got pretty difficult. These folks are so hungry! I ended up helping the available staff run out to the grocery and put together dinner for 35 very hungry adults." Such occurrences are going to be commonplace when the literacy program is on site at shelter and related locations. Instructors will be asked to tolerate constant change.

Instructors at sites away from shelters are hardly immune to the shifting sand of homeless services and policies. Learners who had been attending a survival English class located down the block from their shelter suddenly stopped participating. One particular evening, through a communications mixup and a new staff person, the beds for those men had been given away before they could get back from their class. Not only did attendance drop to zero, but the program was eventually canceled. Programs which send vans or buses to pick up learners and bring them to alternative learning sites can be completely stymied if the rules for length of shelter stay or hours of operation shift. Literacy program success will require instructors who are flexible and who can manage in an uncertain environment over which they have little control.

ABILITY TO COMMUNICATE WITH
SHELTER PROVIDERS

For literacy programs to have any chance at affecting change for learners, no matter how small, those responsible for providing support and shelter for homeless adults must be supportive of that effort. The advocacy organization and especially the director must become convinced of the benefits of literacy instruction for their clients. In most instances, these people are inviting literacy instructors into their establishments and expecting that the instructor "fit in" with their routine. Even with the most meticulous planning and established understandings, however, programs can be undone when the instructor cannot communicate with the provider. Those who offer food and shelter to homeless adults are usually operating on a crisis basis with more people waiting for services than can be handled. Shelter priorities may often not match instructor priorities.

> The instructor arrived at the battered women's shelter at the usual time. She was particularly excited that evening because she was going to work with the young woman who had shown such potential the week before. The instructor had gathered some information for her young learner and was anxious to give it to her. After sitting alone for several minutes in the room set aside for her class, the instructor went out to the kitchen to find out where her students were. "Oh—a local church offered to take them all to a special program this evening! Isn't it wonderful?" she was told. Crestfallen, the instructor was left with her enthusiasm and resources and no students.

While not earth shattering news, such instances indicate the differing viewpoints between shelter providers and instructors.

The instructor felt she was undermined, and the director felt the shelter should not turn down an enriching opportunity.

On a more serious note, it is possible for shelter providers to disagree with the educational plan an instructor and learner might devise. It can become complicated when the instructor hears the dream, and the shelter provider sees the reality. Communication between the two is essential.

ACQUIRING AND SHARING KNOWLEDGE ABOUT THE COMMUNITY

As discussed in a previous chapter, one of the emerging roles of literacy education in services to homeless adults is to function as a bridge between homeless learners and their communities. The literacy instructor must become knowledgeable of area resources for at least three reasons.

First of all, as a resource person with constantly updated information, the instructor develops a role in the total shelter provider network that becomes increasingly valuable in its own right. Homeless adults may have a more immediate need for information than for anything else. Many shelter residents will be entering employment in the area. Others will be entering the world of benefits and need the skills necessary to manage them. As Goodman, Saxe, and Harvey (1991) suggest, information helps homeless adults gain some control over the world outside the shelter.

Second, the literacy instructor may be easing the trauma of homelessness by offering accurate information to people in bad situations. The simplest list of realtors representing the agencies most likely to deal with adults in transition may be a blessing to the homeless adult faced with dim prospects. Finding out how they may keep their children in school or how they may acquire past records may result in some restored sense of power and purpose for homeless adults. Granted, this aspect of literacy instruction is one that has emerged out of necessity and was probably not anticipated except in the broadest sense of coordinating services with other agencies. Nevertheless, it has become a vital part and strength of many homeless literacy projects.

Finally, by becoming knowledgeable about a community's resources, including educational opportunities, the instructor may be instrumental in bringing the learner in contact with supportive environments and people for longer periods of time. Learners are frequently served by a literacy instructor for brief time periods, sometimes lasting just one or two hours. By being knowledgeable enough of area opportunities and linking learners to them, literacy instructors may be the catalyst for a relatively long learner association with an educational environment. Most homeless adults do remain in the same community (Bassuk, 1990; Children's Defense Fund, 1991; Dail, 1990; Goodman, 1991; Hagen, 1987). "Too little time with the learner" need not be the downfall of literacy projects, provided learners know of other possibilities and are encouraged to take advantage of them.

FULFILLING ACCOUNTABILITY REQUIREMENTS TO THE LITERACY PROGRAM

A frequent question asked about potential instructors for ABE programs is, "Are they good with paperwork?" Most federally funded literacy programs have accountability requirements that are both a burden and a necessity. Excellent opportunities to affect change in people's lives—to do the work of literacy education—will be lost if instructors neglect their mandate to maintain accurate records and learner progress documentation. Such requirements were discussed earlier in terms of barriers to programming for homeless adults.

While current funding mechanisms are in place, however, it would seem foolhardy to jeopardize the good energy and exciting results of homeless literacy projects by neglecting the accountability requirement. Maintaining accurate records, (for instance, attendance sheets, enrollment forms, and rosters) can be extremely difficult in the mercurial homeless environments. Program designers will have to work with instructors to plan for the inevitability of the paperwork and to help instructors spend as little time on it as possible.

In her review of adult basic education in North Carolina, Fingeret (1985) observed that "all persons portray record keeping as a response to external demands rather than as an avenue for increasing program effectiveness through thoughtful collection and analysis of information" (p. 178). The record keeping requirements, then, could serve as one method of evaluating the project. According to one state project director, homeless literacy project developers have done a wonderful job educating auditors on the complexities of working with the homeless. Some stringent requirements have at least been relaxed. It is still imperative, however, for instructors to blend their people skills with documentation skills. In the meantime, documentation can be augmented to help both learners and instructors gauge progress.

STAFF DEVELOPMENT

Selecting and training literacy instructors to work with homeless adults has occurred through a combination of strategies. The first has been to employ instructors who have already been teaching in larger literacy programs or have at least completed some form of training program for such work. The second is to bring in people with minimal literacy education experience but substantial experience with homeless adults. These people then complete an instructor training program and assume instructor responsibilities. In many cases, teacher selection has probably had more to do with personality than with teaching skills. "Give me someone who can relate to the people first. I'll turn them into a teacher" is a common sentiment.

Regardless of the route into instruction, teacher first or teacher second, the subject of training is just beginning to be addressed. While much of the knowledge base required of instructors working with homeless adults is the same as that required in more traditional programs, much of it is not. Some adult educators question the traditional knowledge base (Fingeret, 1985) and would likely find it even more inadequate for instructors assigned to such difficult learning environments. Instructors of homeless adults need training that strengthens both their teaching competencies and their strategies for working in multi-troubled environments. This training should encompass at least six areas: (a) literacy instruction; (b) community resources; (c) knowledge of homelessness issues; (d) crisis management; (e) medical issues; and (f) stress management.

Literacy Instruction

In her evaluation of the Adult Basic Education program in North Carolina, Fingeret (1985) proposes literacy instructor training that includes five basic components. These components apply to homeless project instructors as well. The first is an overview of adult basic education that includes a sociocultural perspective of nonliterate adults. The second component would be an introduction to adult learning and developmental theory. Trainees would also study reading, writing, and math instruction, coupled with some theory and research in these areas. Trainees would receive specific training in adult instruction and assessment methods. Finally, they would have an opportunity to review and examine educational materials.

Granted, literacy instructors working within the daily routines of shelters, soup kitchens, and other related locations have their hands full with the ongoing crisis atmosphere that permeates these programs. Their first obligation, however, is to instruct. Solid instructional methods will help ensure positive outcomes for homeless learners. If anything, homeless literacy instructors will need to be *more* informed and educated about instructional methods and issues if for no other reason than the sheer range of learner needs they will experience.

Community Resources

As discussed earlier, literacy instructors will need to be quite knowledgeable about their community and its resources. This knowledge is often acquired on the job as instructors become more and more enmeshed in the survival world of their learners.

Training can be provided that keeps instructors informed of resources, including employment and job training possibilities. Instructors should be included in any area information and referral workshops or projects and offer their own workshops to community agencies interested in strengthening referrals.

Knowledge of Homelessness Issues

Many adult educators had little or no prior experience in working with homeless adults before Stewart B. McKinney funds allowed them to do so. Typically, they approached the task by copying their past efforts to provide literacy education to the more general public. Instructors immediately encountered overwhelming learner problems (U.S. Department of Education, 1989). They were often seeing the combined effects of poverty and homelessness.

Instructor training should include a component that exposes instructors to what homelessness and poverty mean in this society, the latter included because it is the largest predictor of homelessness (Shinn, Knickman, & Weitzman, 1991). Training should focus on the local situation as well, and incorporate information on how the various social agency policies both create and ameliorate problems.

Crisis Management

Placing instructors in homeless environments means placing them in stressful situations where a range of human difficulties will be encountered. Some events will be considered immediate crises. A sudden fight that boils out of control, an epileptic seizure, a visit from the police, or a dinner that doesn't happen when food is not delivered are common events. Personal crises, such as loss of job, family or friend, personal belongings, or a paycheck can take immediate precedence over instruction and leave the instructor grappling for appropriate responses and strategies.

Literacy educators were not dispatched to homeless shelters and other related locations to take the place of social workers and counselors, however desperate the need for these professionals. But they cannot operate in a vacuum and must be prepared to deal with their learners who present a variety of behaviors. Training in crisis management, provided by both experienced shelter personnel and professional counselors, should be a part of the instructors training program.

Medical Issues

Going into people's "homes," no matter how temporary the home is, means going into their daily lives: going into their lives often includes learning about their medical problems. Ropers (1988) reported that in a sample of homeless adults in Los Angeles County almost 40% reported an accident or acute illness within the past two months. Nearly 46% reported deteriorating health since becoming homeless. In addition, 40% reported chronic physical health problems including diabetes, asthma, epilepsy, and cancer. Tuberculosis and HIV infection are present in some shelter situations and have caused great concern in many areas of the country.

Mental illness is prevalent among homeless populations, although researchers caution against assuming mental illness always precedes homelessness (Mowbray, 1985). Instructors will be working with learners who are experiencing mental health difficulties, especially depression (Ropers, 1988). Whether the problems are physical or mental, instructors could benefit from training in these areas while drawing upon the experiences of shelter personnel and health professionals.

Individual Stress Management

In North Carolina's final report to the Department of Education (U.S. Department of Education, 1990b), the following scene is described.

This was just not the place to have class. We had to meet in the hallways and here and there. There was no enclosure for the classroom. Those who were interested came every time, and we had class the best we could, but the majority were just curious and would enroll and never return. Many would disrupt the class —it was noisy all the time—sometimes there were fights—the interruptions for snacks and announcements too frequent. This atmosphere was not conducive to learning. (p. 16)

This scenario is indicative of the tension between instructors and shelter providers, between the hopes for literacy education and its realities, and between the value of going where the people are versus taking them to alternate locations. Late evening hours in relatively dangerous locations, constant turnover of learners and few visible successes, distractions in the learning environment, and feelings of professional isolation all combine to make teaching homeless adults very challenging. Those same problems make working conditions stressful for homeless literacy instructors and require continuing training and support.

In the federal report on the first year of homeless literacy projects, continual training for instructors is recommended (U.S. Department of Education, 1990b). It is suggested because of "the broad range of problems that accompany homelessness" (p. 25). Training should be provided that will help identify what is stressful to instructors and help them manage its effect. Constant support should be provided to instructors throughout their tenure with literacy projects. They will need encouragement, stress management strategies, and opportunities to remove themselves from or make changes in the working environment.

DISCUSSION

Adult basic education practitioners have known for years what a difference the instructor makes in program participation and outcomes. Most often, the ABE instructors have not had to contend with the stressful physical and emotional circumstances that surround homelessness. Neither have they had to be able to respond immediately with instruction covering such a wide range of needs and interests. Instructors of the homeless are not entirely free to set the learning agenda as they are in the regular classroom. Program coordinators will find that it is not sufficient to rely totally on traditional instructor selection and training when the learners are homeless.

As will be noted in the next chapter, considerable expectations are placed on the instructors. Once selected, their training and support are critical components to program success.

CHAPTER 5

Program Design Goals

The primary goal of literacy program directors at the outset of the Stewart B. McKinney funded state initiatives was to find ways to reach homeless adults. Education agencies met with local homeless service providers and mapped out preliminary plans to offer literacy training. The results as well as some emerging issues have been discussed in previous chapters, but it bears repeating that traditional literacy approaches were coming up short when applied to such troublesome human circumstances. Rather than being able to focus on long range plans and goals, most program administrators were dealing with day-to-day program survival in conditions previously unimagined.

Program design goals are now not only possible but practical, since educators and service providers have begun to rely on the literacy education component for filling previously unmet client needs. An examination of past and present efforts reveals the need for at least seven program goals. It is ironic that many literacy advocates have been asking for the same introspection regarding the larger federal and state literacy efforts (Fingeret, 1985; Fox, 1986). The seven goals discussed in this chapter should assist both seasoned and new program developers as they shape their efforts with homeless adults.

ENCOURAGE MORE LEARNER-CENTERED APPROACHES

According to Jurmo (1989b), learner-centered programs "give learners some control in the planning of instructional activities" (p. 29). At the very least, he notes, learners have access to a variety of educational materials and activities developed by other people. At the other end of the continuum, "learners develop topics, materials, and activities on their own or in collaboration with others" (p. 30). Homeless adult learners are probably choosing from a variety of possibilities as a rule rather than as an exception. Having learners develop topics and produce materials on their own, gives them more control over their own learning, makes sense in terms of efficiency, personal development, and social change.

Learner-generated curriculum materials puts the homeless adults' learning in a more meaningful context, and wastes far less of their educational time than using material unrelated or uninteresting. Learners are also provided with "opportunities to set goals, explore options, and develop strategies for meeting goals through active participation" (Jurmo, 1989a, p. 21). Thus these opportunities enhance their personal development. Social change requires from adults critical thinking and analytical skills, the kind of skills that can be encouraged and nourished through learner-centered approaches to instruction. Learner-centered education could allow people to find their voices and reflect critically on the societal and cultural conditions that contribute to their homelessness.

Learner-centered instruction with homeless adults carries with it several more advantages. It may lessen the resistance to participation in "yet another program" if the learners have more control of content. As has been mentioned earlier, homeless adults have little control over many aspects of their lives (Imbimbo & Pfeffer, 1987). They may respond positively to an educational program that not only allows but insists on their input and control.

A sense of ownership in programs that could lead to longer participation and more frequently met goals may be engendered by learner-centered approaches. Feedback to learners would be constant through feedback from each other, from instructors, and, perhaps, from other service providers. Such feedback would be self-affirming. Finally, a learner-centered approach would result in the generation of appropriate learning materials and activities for the groups of adults yet to enter homelessness but destined for the shelters.

Educators who have been working with homeless adults in the most trying of circumstances may believe that learner-centered approaches are fine in nicer learning environments and with learners who will be staying more than a few hours or nights or weeks. Yet in the sense of selecting materials and activities based on their own stated needs, a great degree of learner-centeredness already exists in the homeless literacy programs. Many of the lifeskills units so commonplace in today's programs had their beginnings in learner-requested assistance and certainly reflected immediate needs. More can be done, however, to incorporate learner centered instruction into literacy programs for the homeless.

Three major program variables that come into play when designing instruction for homeless adults are time, location, and subgroup, with the most influential being time. Making instruction more learner-centered when time in a program is very short is a challenge but can be achieved. Learners can select from a variety of instructional options.

Learners can choose the amount of time they participate and whether they want to work alone, with an instructor or volunteer, or with a group of learners. They can choose their own learning objectives, possibly indicated on a brief learning contract, even if they will have only an hour or two with an instructor. Learners can also be given opportunities to pursue instruction during times other than class time if program designers make materials available. The key element is choice.

Strategies for longer term situations include having learners work in groups to identify relevant needs and issues and, subsequently, to explore them. Given sufficient time, learners in transitional programs can create their own curriculum materials and document their own progress. Jurmo (1989a) writes that learners can "identify themes of personal importance to themselves . . . develop their own texts based on those themes . . . and . . . critically analyze texts produced by others" (p. 23).

This process, notes Jurmo (1989a), lays the foundation for "individual or collective action needed to produce positive changes in the situations in which the learners live" (p. 23). A learner-centered strategy that allows homeless adults to examine their concerns and needs takes advantage of Knowles' (1980) contention that "people become ready to learn something when they experience a need to learn it in order to cope more satisfyingly with real life tasks or problems" (p. 44). Instead of exhibiting disinterest in instruction seemingly unrelated to their needs, learners will have the opportunity to select immediately relevant areas of inquiry.

The more learner-centered instruction is, the more the participating learners are involved in the evaluation of current efforts and the planning for new ones. The nature of homelessness has most learners moving on to other shelters, transitional locations, or permanent housing. Rather than lose the expertise and experiences of soon-to-be-gone learners, instructors can involve them in evaluating and planning for incoming homeless adults. Although it might not be specifically their own, incoming homeless adults would at least be considering materials and issues developed by other homeless adults. After they have left shelters, former learners can still be involved if they are contacted and asked how instructional activities did or did not help them after leaving the shelter. Instructional programs would be constantly updated and improved.

Developing learner-centered programming is especially challenging when homeless adults are required to attend certain activities. The notion of "required" flies in the face of the learner-centered concept. Knowles (1980) views adult learners as volunteers in the process, unlike children who are made to attend classes. The broader literacy programs in the United States are nearly all voluntary, and adult educators typically abhor the notion of a literacy class having any remote atmosphere of punishment.

However, organizations and persons providing shelter to homeless adults may feel they have the prerogative of requiring attendance at programs they believe will benefit their residents. The precedent was set some time ago when alcoholic males, for instance, were required to attend Alcoholic Anonymous meetings, or when all residents at a certain shelter had to attend a nightly church service in order to maintain a bed for the night. It is possible to design for some degree of learner-centeredness even in required circumstances by offering attendees more than one program option, by including them in evaluation of the program, and by allowing nonparticipation.

IMPROVE THE CALIBER AND RANGE OF INSTRUCTION

The tendency of literacy educators to bank more on their interactive and counseling skills than on their teaching skills has already been discussed. The danger in neglecting instructional skills is significant. Boraks (1988) writes, "Delivering literacy programs may leave adult learners knowing that people care, but delivering programs which do not teach in the most effective manner may leave adults feeling that they do not have the ability to succeed" (p. 72). Program designers working with homeless adults could easily become so involved in the campaign to reach and keep potential learners that they neglect the need for instructors to have strong teaching skills.

Strategies for improving the caliber of instruction include strengthening the selection process of instructors and providing additional training to them once selected, as discussed in the previous chapter. Program designers will have to monitor instruction closely and ask if learners are achieving their objectives. Other kinds of support will need to be provided to instructors so they can spend more time focusing on instruction and less on the logistical difficulties of working with such a transient population. Strong instruction should always be a program goal, even with projects that are perhaps dealing with the learners who have more personal, social, and economic problems than any other literacy audience.

DOCUMENT LEARNER SUCCESSES AND ALL OTHER PROGRAM OUTCOMES

Learners need to know they are learning, and shelter and other service providers need to see the value of the literacy program. Knowles (1980), in clarifying andragogical theory, writes that "teachers devote energy to helping the adults get evidence for themselves about the progress they are making toward their educational goals" (p. 49). Traditional literacy programs rely on standardized tests, skills tests scores, and successful passage through increasingly difficult instructional material to measure success. Many of these methods will be of little value to instructors seeing learners for brief periods of time. One method used by literacy instructors to ensure learning and documentation of learning during relatively short periods of time is the learning contract. It applies literally to the next one, two, or three hours if necessary. The instructor and the learner agree upon short, obtainable goals. When the goals are met, the instructor signs off on the contract and adds brief comments.

The contract can be very simple:

I _____, will

_____

_____

_____by _____

Learner _____
Instructor _____
Date _____

The completed contract is given to the learner and the instructor maintains a copy on file. If the project is part of a larger shelter program, a copy of the contract may be kept by shelter providers. The significance of such a simple document should not be underestimated when working with adults in crisis.

The supervisor had just arrived at the shelter class site when she saw John L. handing a learning contract to his teacher so she would put it into his folder. "Did you take the contract somewhere?" asked the supervisor. "Oh yes," replied John. "I showed it to my boss. He liked what I was doing." The supervisor glanced again at the contract. It was wrinkled and folded and somewhat worse for wear after traveling in John's pocket. On the contract, John had agreed to complete two pages of fractions and complete

two sections in a reading book. He had completed the contract
and his instructor had signed it. The supervisor couldn't figure
out what item was most significant to John: seeing his name,
seeing his name associated with the community college, seeing
his instructor's signature, or knowing that he had been successful.

Documents take on major significance to homeless adults for
whom possession, loss, and re-acquisition of identification and
records is an ongoing struggle. That particular document, the
learning contract, showed that John existed.

At the end of the instructional session, the instructor is able
to compile information on dozens of learner accomplishments
and successes. By putting all the documents together, the program coordinator is able to ascertain that learning is going on,
that successes are many, and that certain subject areas are of
frequent interest to homeless adults. It is not stretching the truth
to say that earlier program efforts involved enormous energy
devoted to simply reaching homeless adults but much less energy
on documenting learning.

Many literacy programs nationally are focusing on competency-based approaches to basic skills training and have adopted
various assessment tools and accountability mechanisms. Regardless of the methods—from a simple contract to a more sophisticated, longer range assessment and measurement approach
—literacy program developers must take great care to be ac-
countable to their learners. In the words of a project analyst
working with one state's homeless literacy project, "Is learning
going on there? How do you know?"

PLAN FOR MULTIPLE POINTS OF ENTRY INTO THE LEARNING PROCESS

Homeless shelter residents are usually not thinking about
improving their literacy skills, although some shelter providers
believe they should be. The residents are not unlike other adults
who fail to see improving their literacy skills as a key to change.

Even if they did see that need, they have many other problems to face that take on daily survival proportions in importance.

Engaging potential learners in educational activities requires multiple points of entry into the learning process both within the shelter or other teaching environment and within the community. A single approach, such as offering a GED preparation hour a couple of nights a week, will serve the needs of some residents but leave out many more who could benefit from a broader range of instructional offerings. In homeless shelters, soup kitchens, motels, day labor pickup sites, racetracks, Indian reservations, and makeshift learning labs, instructors are attempting to issue the invitation to learn in as many ways as possible.

> On a typical day at a shelter which serves battered women, a variety of instructional areas are activated. Sharon A. has picked up a GED practice book left on site by the instructor and is waiting to ask what will be involved if she decides to start the process of working toward getting a GED. Robin M. has chosen to work on her reading skills and is going to show the instructor her completed assignments in a reading workbook. Kaye L. observed people last week working on their math skills using an audio-cassette program. Today, she would like to try it too. Flora R. is reaching the end of her six-week stay and must find an apartment in the next two weeks. She wants to complete a lifeskills unit on the subject and has noted a couple of other units that interest her as well.

Such flexibility on the part of the instructional program makes it easier for shelter providers to include literacy education in their overall program. Multiple points of entry, in turn, make it easier for homeless adults to choose their manner of participation. One particular shelter operates both an emergency shelter and a transitional program for men who have substance abuse problems. Each participant in the latter group has worked out a set of goals with the program counselor that includes an educational plan. Some of these plans include studying for and getting the GED, getting started on learning to read, seeking better employment, brushing up on math skills, or pursuing a postsecondary program in the area. The homeless literacy project instructors work with each participant toward meeting their stated goals, and progress is monitored closely by all involved. By offering multiple entry points, the literacy program was able to become highly relevant to both learners and shelter staff. When, in earlier efforts, the program was perceived as being only for nonreaders, very few learners participated.

Another application of a multiple entry points strategy comes with providing a broad array of program options throughout the community. These options serve as a welcome to homeless adult learners. Alternative sites can be developed or existing ones can be made more friendly and accessible to the homeless person. A referral network can be established that keeps homeless adults and service providers informed as to the whereabouts of class sites that are particularly appropriate for homeless learners.

PLAN FOR MULTIPLE POINTS OF STAYING

A common concern voiced by state after state as they began taking literacy education to homeless adults was the rapid turnover of learners. In the U.S. Department of Education (1990a) report that followed the first year's efforts, a key recommendation was that learners somehow have longer periods of time to complete their educational goals. Longer residential stability would, of course, make a considerable difference in what literacy programs could accomplish. However, unless the literacy program directors choose to serve only those adults who live in more transitional settings, the realities of transience remain. Yet, this transience is an obstacle to educational progress that can be partly overcome by planning for multiple points of staying.

One strategy is to refer the homeless adult to other program sites in the immediate area that would be especially appropriate for their circumstances. In one instance, a regular literacy class site was developed in the downtown area that was also near several homeless shelters. The site was designed to include child care. The instructor chosen for the site had an extensive background in social services in the area and was aware of an assortment of support possibilities for her learners. As a result, homeless men and women as well as nearly homeless learners frequent the site. They either supplement their shelter work with homeless literacy instructors or attend the new site after leaving the shelter. It is possible for some homeless adults to spend nine or ten hours a week working on their educational objectives.

> Jackie M., a single woman with two pre-school children, first encountered literacy instruction when she was staying at an emergency facility. She talked with the onsite instructor about her desire to get her GED. Her instructor urged Jackie to take advantage of two other class sites while she had some support and a little time. For several weeks, Jackie worked with the shelter instructor one morning a week. Then she attended a nearby site which offered child care two afternoons a week. And one evening a week, Jackie attended a special homeless adult literacy project located at an inner city church. Transportation and child care were provided. Eventually, when Jackie left the shelter and acquired an apartment in public housing, she began attending a literacy program located one block from her home.

Adults do move from shelter to shelter. Yet, instructors can make every effort to connect learners to different programs. This strategy is especially significant when the learners have begun pursuing beginning reading instruction. With coordination, it is possible to expand the available time frame for instruction. Documentation and tracking are both very difficult, but instructors working closely together can overcome these obstacles. Providing for multiple points of staying and managing the necessary coordination may be especially difficult for programs in rural areas which do not have many options for the learner.

INVOLVE SHELTER STAFF AND OTHER SERVICE PROVIDERS IN PROGRAM PLANNING AND IMPLEMENTATION

Literacy programs for the homeless should not operate in isolation and should seek shelter provider support. This support can range from allowing the literacy instructors access to shelter residents all the way to incorporating the literacy program into the daily shelter routine and program. The meaning of "access" is as varied as every other homeless issue. Access according to one shelter provider may mean allowing the instructor to set a teacher's box on a dining room table after dinner is cleaned up and make an announcement, "The instructor is here tonight for any of you who want to study." "Access" to a soup kitchen director may be something entirely different.

> Every week, several dozen homeless men and women lined up at the soup kitchen for lunch. Seeing an opportunity to reach the people, the literacy project staff asked the soup kitchen director what they believed to be a reasonable request. "Can we come in at lunch time and work with the homeless adults? We have this wonderful program . . . " The quick response was, "absolutely not." The supervisor explained that every program attempting to provide services to the homeless—the health department, Social Security, the Employment office, substance abuse programs—wanted to come in at lunch. But she wanted her diners to come in, eat in peace, and leave. Access to the soup kitchen was denied.

Some weeks thereafter, the social services director from a huge, old downtown church located across the street from the soup kitchen called the literacy project coordinator. "Everyday," she said, "we have several homeless men come in here before or after lunch and ask for clothing from our clothes closet. Usually they are Latin Americans and speak no English. What can your project do to help these men? We'll give you the space you need at our church."

Now, two mornings a week, a literacy teacher who is originally from Guatemala stands on the sidewalk next to the soup kitchen. As the homeless adults line up for lunch, she is able to direct them to the church across the street. When she speaks in Spanish with some of the men, almost without fail several learners approach her just as eager for survival English as they are for lunch. The soup kitchen director now actively refers people to the literacy program in the church across the street. The combined effort of service providers at the soup kitchen, the local church, and the literacy program resulted in a valuable program for perhaps the most educationally needy homeless adults of all.

Shelter programs vary enormously in terms of clientele, length of stay, degree of crisis, and operating philosophies. They also vary in their commitments to or understanding of literacy education. While most service providers would probably rank literacy education high on the list of long-term client needs, the circumstances in their shelters preclude the commitment they would like learners to make. Program developers will have to devise several strategies in order to have access to learners. For instance, transportation and child care can be designed into project grants so that learners who otherwise would not be able to come can attend educational activities.

Shelter providers most often cannot offer the services themselves but will be supportive of literacy efforts if they are provided by someone else. Program designer and instructor efforts could include participating in various coalitions and working groups that gather providers together for exchange of ideas and circulate, through newsletters, information on a regular basis. Perhaps the most effective strategy for maintaining access to learners is to constantly show the shelter providers that the literacy program is making a difference in homeless people's lives. Even with the best of circumstances and all possible support provided, program directors will usually have to rely on the support of the people who administer the homeless programs and operate the shelters. The literacy program will either have guest status or have "one more program in the midst of many" status.

CREATE COMMUNITY PARTNERSHIPS THAT BROADEN THE SCOPE OF EDUCATIONAL AND SOCIAL OPPORTUNITIES FOR LEARNERS

In the sometimes chaotic, complex, and changing world of homelessness, the effort to provide literacy skills to adults who need them may seem minuscule. The instructors, while delighted with individual accomplishments of learners, are always working "downstream," where, as Egan (1984) describes it, helpers are working with clients already "involved in malfunctioning systems without being able to do anything about the system or systems that are contributing to their clients' problems" (p. 23). A design strategy that broadens the potential impact of the literacy effort involves connecting learners to community resources.

At a primary level, many instructors are already serving this function. As previously discussed, literacy education programs for homeless adults are serving the role of resource linkage between learners and the community at large. Locally oriented resource guides have been developed, with some of them in more than one language. The guides are used as part of lifeskills units as well.

Another strategy is to become a partner in the development of community-oriented programs. This can be done in the sense of encouraging collaborative efforts rather than isolating learners and serving them through an assortment of agencies. The literacy program, for instance, can serve as an anchor that holds down a larger program. For example, a community action agency's outreach program joined with the local homeless literacy project and the local women's center to provide programming to homeless adults from several area shelters.

Because of combined resources and shared responsibilities, the collaborative program was able to provide transportation and child care, to offer lifeskills and traditional literacy instruction, to recruit and train volunteers from all over the community, and to regularly bring in resource people to help the participants deal with several issues. The partners in the project met regularly to discuss successes and weaknesses and to maintain a valuable educational service for as many as 25 adults per evening session.

DISCUSSION

Literacy practitioners working with homeless adults have demonstrated they can reach the homeless population and provide meaningful instruction. The day-to-day concerns will still consume project time and demand ongoing program adjustments. At this point, though, it is possible to focus attention on longer range instructional and program goals. The next chapter will offer specific instructional models that will help educators meet their goals.

CHAPTER 6

Program Design Models

Traditional ABE literacy programs are scattered about cities and counties in a combination of community schools and centers, college campuses, churches, libraries, workplaces, corrections institutions, mental and medical hospitals, group homes, and senior citizens centers. However, the actual format and curriculum are generally the same from one site to another, although specific curriculum materials might vary with adaptations being made to fit the need. Considerable energy has been devoted throughout the homeless literacy projects to reach out to homeless adults instead of waiting for them to select and, subsequently, attend classes at the more typical program sites in a community. When providing literacy education for homeless adults, the site itself takes on major significance and, in many ways, drives the program.

One reason is that different shelters take in different subsets of the homeless population, and, as a result, immediate needs will differ dramatically from shelter to shelter. The sites, especially those located at shelters, offer varying degrees of environmental appropriateness for learning. Program design is dictated in many ways by the size and nature of the space available and, as discussed in a previous chapter, by the rules and regulations of the shelter. In thinking about program models, then, it is useful to frame them in terms of location.

Six models are described in this chapter that are variations of the onsite or offsite plans. The onsite models provide instruction where homeless people live and sleep, however temporarily. The usual onsite locations include emergency shelters, semi-transitional shelters, and transitional shelters. The definition can extend to areas beneath bridges and race tracks. Offsite locations are often places frequented by homeless people such as soup kitchens, day labor pickup sites, libraries, churches, and social service agencies. In some instances, offsite locations are housed at more formal designated learning areas such as public schools, community colleges, and off-campus or community-sponsored learning centers. Homeless adults in each instance either go to offsite locations on their own or are provided with transportation and, very often, child care.

Other program distinctions include participation, curriculum, and duration. In some cases, participation is voluntary, and in others it is required. Participants may be members of a specific subgroups such as mothers with children or men with substance abuse problems. Program areas, or as Knowles (1980) describes the situation, "problem areas," commonly include traditional ABE instruction and GED preparation, lifeskills, readiness activities, survival English, transactions, and educational counseling. Practitioners usually use the term, "ABE/GED," to mean the range of instruction that starts with beginning readers and goes through preparation for the GED examination. Materials are designed to move learners through increasingly difficult exercises and take them to higher levels of comprehension.

The term "lifeskills" is broadly applied to skill areas other than the ABE/GED traditional literacy subjects of reading, writing, speaking, computing, and problem solving. They are a combination of immediately useful topics and planned basic skills improvements. For example, a lifeskills topic could be "Finding Employment." Throughout the activities in the lifeskills module will be vocabulary practice, writing exercises, and opportunities to reflect upon and solve problems about gaining employment.

Lifeskills approaches to literacy education teach basic skills in the context of immediately relevant information. The concept is dynamic and in process with new units being developed to meet immediate needs as they arise. In some instances, topics such as goal setting, self esteem, and getting organized are included under the lifeskills umbrella. Materials are sometimes produced locally and supplemented by a variety of published sources.

Survival English encompasses the language skills needed immediately by non-English-speaking homeless adults. Basic vocabulary, particularly as it relates to current needs such as acquiring identification, getting health care, and dealing with immigration issues forms the content areas for instruction. In some situations, participants may study basic English.

Readiness activities prepare learners for life changes. Examples include job readiness or pre-employment training, study skills, basic food preparation as it relates to restricted budgets, homemaking, and career exploration. Some programs may include these areas under the lifeskills designation.

Two remaining areas are generally part of all homeless adult education activities regardless of curriculum focus. The first is assistance with transactions. This involves providing assistance with written tasks and tasks requiring reading comprehension. Homeless adults sometimes need assistance with the various forms required by social service, health, and housing agencies. Also, many homeless adults are eligible for Social Security benefits and need assistance coping with the requirements. The second area, educational counseling, takes place in nearly all homeless literacy programs as instructors serve their connecting role between the learner and community education resources.

The most critical factor other than location is time. How long will learners be participating in the literacy program? The six models presented here may each involve learners who will attend a program for one evening or several months. Even in the more transitional programs where adults stay for at least two months, learners may suddenly leave the shelter when they think they are getting on their feet. The varying lengths of educational tenure require constant diligence on the part of instructors and program designers in order to maximize learning opportunities and to document results. The objectives of literacy programs are always shaped and affected by the length of time learners will have to participate in instruction. The program design models offered in this chapter are operational within any length of learner tenure.

MODEL 1: RESOURCE TEACHER ONSITE

The Resource Teacher Model may be the most frequent application of literacy education for homeless adults. Quite simply, an instructor is placed at the shelter site on a regularly scheduled basis and is available for those learners who request instruction or assistance. A routine setup would have the instructor available after dinner, although other hours may be involved. Shelter residents are informed of the instructor's presence and are encouraged to participate. They may choose the content that interests them and also the extent of their involvement. The instructor uses whatever space may be available and offers ABE/GED, lifeskills, readiness activities, and survival English, as well as transactions assistance and educational counseling. Assessment of learners is done most often by asking and by other informal means that are nonobtrusive and quick.

The Resource Teacher Model lends itself well to even the most temporary of shelter situations. One drawback, however, is the brevity of tenure and subsequent difficulty in documenting educational objectives and achievement. The simple learning contract works well in this model and provides immediate feedback. The Resource Teacher Model also involves frequent referrals and assistance with transactions. This model expands its potential when learners begin attending other literacy classes in the area because of initial exposure in this setting.

MODEL 2: THE WORKSHOP MODEL

Some shelter programs such as those at battered women's shelters incorporate lifeskills and readiness workshops into the shelter schedule. The homeless literacy project provides the workshop instruction as requested by shelter personnel. For example, a series of workshops offered at a transitional shelter might cover topics such as finding apartments and employment, locating suitable child care, helping children in school, and managing money. Readiness workshops such as those covering pre-employment skills or self esteem issues may also be offered through this model. Attendance may or may not be required. Certificates can be awarded upon completion of part or all of the series.

The Workshop Model allows each shelter to bring in relevant educational programming with a minimum of program development or staffing. It gives educators a point of contact with homeless adults and opportunities to refer them to other programs. Instructors can draw from other resources in the area and supplement their own efforts. For instance, a lifeskills unit on legal issues can be bolstered by a visit from an area attorney. Other areas of concern such as helping children in school can be supported by visits from local school personnel.

Difficulties with this model come in the form of support services, available space for instruction, and the relevance of the instruction. Onsite workshops should be accompanied by child care if they are taking place in family shelters. The learning space needs to be away from other traffic and activities. Finally, the instructor must work very closely with shelter staff and residents to offer learning activities that fit the realities of people's lives and immediate needs.

For instance, a budgeting workshop may have the ingredients thought necessary by shelter staff but be far removed from the immediate experience of the participants. Also, what is perceived to be a need by shelter staff and instructors may not be perceived that way by shelter residents (Imbimbo & Pfeffer, 1987). The assumption that young women with children perceive the need for improved parenting skills, for example, may be aimed towards residents who believe parenting is what they do best. A workshop on parenting skills would have to be designed so that participants drive the content rather than be expected to receive it from others.

MODEL 3: THE INTEGRATED MODEL

This onsite model is probably the ideal onsite application of literacy education for homeless adults. Its existence represents a dynamic blend of shelter philosophy and instructional relevance. While some shelter efforts are designed primarily to provide the basic needs of homeless people without frills, other programs are much more comprehensive. The shelter program, in a sense, is something one does over a period of time and it is designed to move people along a continuum between dependence and independence. This movement may involve alcohol treatment and counseling, work with vocational rehabilitation agencies, support group meetings, and threading the intricacies of social service bureaucracies.

The shelter program, using a case management or case plan approach, includes an educational component that can be designed by the homeless literacy project. The literacy instructor helps residents meet the educational goals they have established for themselves. For instance, a shelter resident may desire to pursue the GED examination. Another may need to improve budgeting skills. Progress is recorded and monitored by both instructors and responsible shelter staff.

In the Integrated Model, the instructor is viewed as a participant in the overall shelter program and part of the team, and as such is included in staff discussions and planning sessions. The residents' attendance at instructional sessions is constantly encouraged by all involved and is rewarded in as many ways as possible. Paid or volunteer advocates assist instructors and perform such services as personally accompanying shelter residents to appointments and testing dates.

This model functions best when learners are involved for several weeks or months with instructors. It may be possible for learners to attend additional classes in the area and thus maximize training opportunities. Upon completion of such a program, learners will have accumulated a portfolio of certificates, learning contracts, tests results, and other evidence of learning. If they are involved in seeking employment or getting accepted into training programs, they may use the ongoing documentation to boost their chances for success outside the shelter. The integrated approach features constant positive feedback to the learners from all parties involved.

Of all the onsite models, the Integrated Model demands the most delicate balance between the literacy program objectives and the shelter program objectives. Theories of personal growth may differ, and educators may disagree with the operating philosophy of a particular shelter. The integrated approach is especially sensitive to even the slightest shift in staff attitude or staff changes. Finally, the integrated approach is very demanding on instructors who will be involved in high levels of documentation and who will face the additional demands of routine staff meetings. These activities may take the instructor outside the remunerative contract period.

All onsite models have to adapt to the instructional barriers discussed in Chapter 1. These models are very dependent upon shelter staff support and because of these programs have been known to disintegrate overnight. The onsite models need instructors who can function both as part of a team and as an integral connective point for the learners. The "kitchen syndrome" can prevail with onsite models. This is a way of describing what happens when instruction is literally taking place in peoples' kitchens, living and dining rooms, and sleeping quarters. There are clothes to be washed, meals to be cleared, phone calls to be made, letters to be read, spills to be cleaned up, and children to be bathed. Caseworkers may be asking their clients to appear in their offices at certain times, which disrupts ongoing instruction. In spite of these difficulties, however, the onsite models take instruction to the learners, afford them a wide latitude of instructional choices, and connect them in some way to the community at large. A point of contact with education is made possible that otherwise might never have occurred.

MODEL 4: RESOURCE MODEL OFFSITE

Sometimes instruction for homeless adults works best away from the shelter environment. Also, many homeless adults do not stay in shelters but will be found in area locations such as soup kitchens or day shelters. Instruction may be offered at a day labor pickup site, a local church, or a downtown library. Instructional content may be very specific, such as survival English. It may also be more general and similar to the onsite Resource

Teacher Model. Instructors can anticipate doing a great deal of screening and referral work and transactions assistance. Basic lifeskills such as map reading and negotiating bus schedules may be offered. As always with homeless literacy projects, instruction will be as dynamic and changing as the learners themselves.

A day shelter location holds particular promise for the offsite Resource Teacher Model. The instructor can establish rapport with the clientele and begin to develop instruction that meets their expressed needs. A referral board can be set up by the literacy project that focuses on area learning opportunities and encourages continuing community connections. If possible, the literacy instructor can monitor a telephone which potential learners might use for seeking employment. The use of the phone can become an entree into further instructional activities.

The offsite Resource Teacher Model certainly has its share of difficulties. A soup kitchen may simply not have instructional space available or allow for instructional time past the meal hours. Some offsite locations are in dangerous areas. Others are in environments not very conducive to learning or to learner privacy. In some instances, literacy instructors could find themselves "in charge" where largely volunteer-driven operations suddenly have no one present who has any authority. Program developers have to weigh the potential benefits to homeless adult learners against the problems of working in difficult-to-control learning environments.

MODEL 5: LEARNING CENTER OFFSITE

This model involves transporting shelter residents to some type of learning center away from the shelter environment. In some instances, the bus or van driver is also a counselor. Usually, this model follows the traditional ABE/GED format with some inclusion of lifeskills and readiness activities. Much emphasis is placed on assessment of learner skills and subsequent progression through basic skills instruction. The Learning Center Model allows educators to have access to more sophisticated educational technologies such as computer-assisted instruction and audio or video based learning. Child care is often a component of the Learning Center Model and possibilities exist for intergenerational literacy activities.

The transportation component of the Learning Center Model certainly can take on a life of its own very quickly. Programs using this model to serve homeless adults struggle with the financial ramifications of owning or leasing vans, maintaining them, and covering insurance costs. Another drawback to this Learning Center Model is the relative isolation of the instructors from the day-to-day world of the homeless learner and the lack of opportunity to develop trusting relationships with them. These drawbacks may be more than compensated for, however, by the provision of an unimpeded learning environment. Also, volunteers may be more interested in working at learning centers than at shelters which may be located in unsafe areas of the community. Finally, the learners may be much happier working in a more formal learning environment instead of trying to learn in the public spaces of shelters and soup kitchens.

MODEL 6: COMMUNITY-BASED PARTNERSHIPS

The preceding models, while dependent upon cooperative arrangements, are not necessarily working partnerships. A partnership model divides the responsibilities and multiplies the energies. Literacy providers can enter into relationships with other organizations that work with similar clientele and greatly expand their capabilities of reaching homeless adults. For example, a church-based community outreach organization can join forces with the homeless literacy project and develop comprehensive programming that would be beyond the reach of either partner alone.

The essential elements of the Community-Based Partnership Model are (a) that all partners contribute some combination of time, money, and other resources; (b) that all partners participate in program planning and evaluation; (c) that all partners tap their unique community resources such as volunteers and people willing to donate to the program in some manner; (d) that all partners provide linkages between learners and the community at large; and (e) that all partners involve the learners in the planning and implementation of the program. A Community-Based Partnership allows the literacy program the luxury of not standing alone, of sharing responsibilities, and of having its efforts supported.

One difficulty with the Community-Based Partnership Model comes with the dynamics of partnerships. The joint enterprise does not operate on a kind of "automatic pilot." Great sensitivity to people and organizations is required to maintain the positive energy needed to drive the partnership. The partners must maintain their commitment to serve homeless adults while also meeting their respective organization's goals and requirements. Misunderstandings occur easily, and interpretations of divisions of labor can change. The support services required to bring learners to the Community-Based Partnership program involve constant diligence and maintenance. The bigger the partnership, the stronger the likelihood that logistical mistakes will occur. Finally, problems can arise when individual organizations share differing views on appropriate approaches to homeless adult education. Honesty and openness in communication are absolutely necessary.

DISCUSSION

Across the nation, programs are developing that stretch the descriptions of these six models and, perhaps, add additional models. For instance, one effort offers an external degree program to homeless adults living in transitional housing that is located in a converted motel. An instructor takes lessons to the participants and picks up completed assignments so they can be graded at another location. New lessons are left with the learners. The educational process in this case is a combination of onsite and offsite models. The program models are being wonderfully enhanced by a range of readiness activities that include improvisational theater and publishable writing projects.

In spite of various kinds of barriers, literacy programs are being developed that combine the different kinds of models in ways that offer multiple points of access to thousands of homeless adults. All models allow literacy programs for homeless adults to fulfill the roles that have developed over the years. The programs provide basic skills, GED, and lifeskills training. They provide assistance with transactional activities and educational counseling. And the programs serve as a link between learners and their communities and between learners and themselves.

CHAPTER 7

Program Planning and Evaluation

A review of adult basic education literature reveals a variety of program evaluation methods and purposes (Fingeret, 1985; Fischer & Evanson, 1979). It is difficult to talk about evaluation, however, without first talking about program planning and goal setting. Padak and Padak (1991), in discussing how to improve literacy program evaluations, believe that "evaluation guidelines should be established when programs are planned, and the program's goals should direct the nature of the evaluation" (p. 376).

Homeless literacy project designers have had to devote considerable energy to their primary goal of reaching the clientele. Clarity on program goals has often come after the fact, after placing instructors in shelters, after developing curriculum materials that are relevant to situations, after experiencing instructor strengths and weaknesses, and after dealing with constantly changing environments. Just as several roles for literacy education with homeless adults have evolved after two or three years of experimentation, so has the need for program planning and evaluation. This chapter will briefly examine each of these areas.

GETTING STARTED WITH PROGRAM PLANNING

As educators begin to develop a literary program for the homeless they must consider first what is known about the learner and the learner's needs. Then program planners must determine how homeless learners best learn; finally educators must consider the practical aspects of how to make the program work.

Knowing the Learner

Vella (1989), in discussing educational program planning, notes the importance of determining who will be served and why. This corresponds to the University of the State of New York's (1990) contention that "knowing who you are serving and what they seek when entering adult literacy classes is of the utmost importance in planning an effective program" (p. 5). Early reports from the initial literacy providers revealed surprises at the tremendous diversity and wide ranging needs of the homeless population (U.S. Department of Education, 1990a).

Educators were surprised also at the lack of experience many homeless parents had in living independently and at the similarities between working with homeless families and working with those living in public housing areas. Educators also were perplexed with the inner workings of the shelter provider system and personnel. This last point reflects one of the challenges particular to literacy education for the homeless. Knowing one's audience means knowing both the homeless learners and those who provide for them. Both are so intertwined that to ignore the latter is to sabotage program efforts from the outset.

Three strategies for learning more about the population to be served begin with reading the available literature on homelessness. Much of the literature is descriptive (Ropers, 1988; Hagen, 1987). As is true with literature about adult basic education, considerable interest in the personal characteristics of homeless adults is evident. The mental health aspects of homelessness have been frequently described (Drake, Osher, & Wallach, 1991; General Accounting Office, 1988; Levine & Rog, 1990). Family homelessness has commanded considerable attention (Bassuk & Rosenberg, 1988, Children's Defense Fund, 1991; Shinn, Knickman, & Weitzman, 1991). Other authors have examined the significance of losing one's home (Fried, 1963; Rivlin, 1990), and the need for psychological intervention that deals with the trauma of homelessness (Goodman, Saxe, & Harvey, 1991). The challenge for the adult educator is to examine the literature in terms of implications for adult learners rather than to categorize people into subgroups.

The second strategy is to meet with area shelter providers and others offering services to homeless adults. Literacy educators or their sponsoring education agencies have historically not been viewed as part of the programmatic process in serving homeless adults. Seeking information about homeless adults in the area and about the structure of local services allows the literacy educator to gain entry into the process while also gathering information. Many communities have working groups, task forces, and coalitions dealing with particular aspects of homelessness. Program designers will want to become involved, at least as observers, in such groups to learn more about homeless people and their service networks. In all instances, the literacy program designer should be seeking information that will help shape the program's mission.

The third strategy involves speaking directly with homeless adults. Gaining access to current or formerly homeless adults will require an invitation from shelter and service providers. They will likely have privacy concerns and some wariness about yet another program set up to help homeless individuals. A program designer can ask to observe other programs in operation, such as parenting classes or a theater project. When possible, the designer may be able to speak with shelter residents or homeless adults who frequent clinics, mobile health vans, or other support service locations. The purpose is to get acquainted with the population and to develop a sense for homeless adults as learners who bring considerable personal strengths with them (Koegel, Burnam, & Farr, 1990).

After learning "who" might be participating in the literacy project, it is time to examine the learning needs and interests of homeless adults. Vella (1989) believes this involves naming the situation that calls for the program, or formulating the "why." Why do homeless adults need the literacy program? What can it offer them? They can be asked about their needs and interests through personal interviews, group discussions, and questionnaires.

Social service agency personnel as well as various advocacy groups, health care providers, and funding agencies can speak to the literacy related needs of the homeless people they serve. Shelter providers will likely have firsthand knowledge of the literacy needs of their residents. Employers who have worked with homeless adults can be asked what they perceive as educational needs of their homeless workers. Personnel at hospital emergency rooms can be a good source of information on educational needs. Literacy program designers must be cautious, however, in balancing what shelter providers and others perceive as instructional needs of homeless adults and what the adults themselves express as their educational goals.

Reviewing the Research

While very little has been written about the homeless adult as a learner, educators can extrapolate from existing research and come up with implications for instruction. Reviewing research on homelessness through the lens of the *homeless adult learner* will serve to focus the adult educator toward strategies of collaboration, respect, and participation (Chavis, Stucky, & Wandersman, 1983). The view of the homeless adult learner should be based on strengths, not deficits (Caplan & Nelson, 1973). Since so much of the literature about homelessness focuses on subgroups and their problems, it is easy to take the deficit perspective.

Shinn (1991) and others have questioned much of the research that attributes causes of homelessness to personal deficiencies such as mental illness, social isolation, and substance abuse. They stress the possibility that these social problems are consequential to homelessness. Educators want to avoid the "fix the deficiency" approach and focus instead on providing opportunities that build on learner strengths. Many homeless people have shown amazing resilience, good organizational skills, and enormous pride in their accomplishments (Koegel, Burnam, & Farr, 1990). The deficit approach has been harmful to the broader literacy program efforts nationally (Fingeret, 1989), and would be equally harmful, if not even more harmful, to homeless adults who are already struggling to exist.

Practical Considerations

Some additional guidelines include assessing available support services, selecting program staff, and reviewing and selecting curriculum materials (University of the State of New York, 1990). The provision of transportation and child care have proven to be essential for program success and, in most cases, should be planned from the outset. Selecting sensitive and instructionally competent instructors, supporting them after they begin teaching, and challenging them to seek innovation is critical. Quite often the literacy program for the homeless, in many ways, IS the instructor.

Another component of the New York model is to review and select curriculum materials. Program planners should take advantage of existing lifeskills curricula (Stuart, 1990; Kansas Board of Education, 1990). These contain topics already known to be of interest to homeless adults. Materials designed specifically for a particular community, such as a resource guide, may be necessary. Another valuable source of information for program planners is other homeless literacy projects. Sharing resources, experiences, and methods and curriculum materials builds strength for all the programs.

Homeless literacy projects will reflect the operational policies of the larger literacy enterprise that is sponsoring them. Some programs may have to operate under the same attendance rules as the broader literacy program. If a minimum of eight students is required to maintain a paid instructor, for instance, it would make little sense to focus efforts on small transitional settings that have just a few families or individuals in residence at any given time. In these situations, a program might be planned that transports individuals from several sites and takes them to a central location.

Hopefully, the literacy program should be allowed to grow into its challenges and not have to start serving too many locations at once. Planners can select a model that is appropriate to the circumstances. They can take those first steps toward more comprehensive coverage or multiple points of entry into the learning process. Keeping in mind the constantly changing homeless shelter environments, the shifting homeless populations, and the sensitivity of even the most thought-out programs to any change at all, the program planner will do well to work closely and continuously with one or two sites before expanding.

Documentation of learning should begin the very first day of operation. Documentation has been discussed earlier in this volume and will not be elaborated upon at this point. Program planners must keep in mind that the ultimate purpose of the homeless literacy program is to provide opportunities for homeless adults to learn. It is not enough to assume learning is going on—not enough for the learner, the supportive community, or the sponsoring organization. Documentation should be considered and planned for as a forethought, not a hindsight.

SELECTING AND EVALUATING
PROGRAM GOALS

Padak and Padak (1991) note that the first requirement for literacy program evaluation is that it be based on the stated goals of the program. The initial goal of the first homeless literacy project directors was to connect with homeless adults. The second goal was to maintain that connection. Since those beginning efforts, a bank of information and insights has led to broader ranging program goals. As is true with adult basic education programs in general, homeless literacy programs are each going to reflect the uniqueness of their particular communities, sponsoring educational agencies, and homeless populations. One set of program goals may not be totally appropriate for a different project.

Knowles (1980) believes adult education should be "a process of facilitating and providing resources for self-directed inquiry and development" (p. 201). Several goals that are more in line with the wider needs of homeless adults have emerged since the initiation of the homeless literacy programs. These can guide the practitioner charged with developing new programs or examining ongoing projects.

These goals include the following:

1. Offering homeless adults the opportunity to further use and develop their literacy skills in order to meet their immediate learning needs

2. Inviting homeless adult learners into the instructional process in as many ways as possible, thereby providing multiple points of entry

3. Expanding the instructional time frame for each learner, so that the learner can remain involved in education longer than a brief shelter stay would permit

4. Providing as many opportunities as possible for the homeless learner to make contact with other community programs that can continue providing support

5. Providing documented evidence to the learner, to shelter providers, and to the sponsoring education agency that learning is actually taking place

6. Maintaining cooperative agreements and working partnerships with other agencies in the community serving homeless adults

These goals are focused primarily on the learner. But they also require ongoing efforts to maintain old and develop new working relationships within the community. As the role of literacy education in services to homeless adults continues to expand, so will the goals of these literacy projects.

Knowles (1980) suggests that a starting point in program evaluation is "a good question that can be answered by data" (p. 205). Formulating the questions, however, can be troublesome. Evaluation in adult basic education has traditionally been a struggle. Willing (1989) points out four reasons for this problem, each of which is applicable to homeless adult education. First of all, program administrators often have many other responsibilities that are time consuming. Second, ABE classes are typically scattered all around a community and meet at all hours of the day and evening. Third, most instructors are part time and have little background in adult education. Fourth, instructional variety is expanding as the definitions of literacy broaden, which makes evaluation a difficult task.

Padak and Padak (1991) assert that the routine adult literacy policy of open-entry and open-exit classes where students may enter or leave at any time makes evaluation extremely challenging. In spite of these challenges, program evaluation helps educators improve future planning; program evaluation benefits current practices as well. Evaluation of homeless literacy projects in particular is critical if participants are to get maximum gain from their involvement, however brief, with the program.

Reviewing evaluation efforts in adult basic education, Fingeret (1985) notes that "researchers have tended to isolate outcomes rather than attempting to understand the interaction between program, student, and environment" (p. 14). Outcomes related to economics, personal and social changes, and citizenship are typical. Homeless project coordinators are asked to report on academic progress, employment changes, and transitions out of homelessness. As Fingeret observes, evaluation studies in adult basic education have seldom been designed to illuminate the internal processes and dynamics of programs. What impact did the literacy program have on the learners, according to the learners themselves?

Evidence of internal processes has most often been supplied in the form of anecdotal evidence or success stories. But these reports are not systematic. They tend to ignore the learners for whom the program had no appreciable impact, a negative impact, or an outcome that would be personally meaningful but that fails to fit into expected goals. It is possible to address both educational outcomes and personal meaningfulness. Fingeret and Danin (1991) evaluated the Literacy Volunteers of New York City program using a combination of quantitative and qualitative techniques. The research question agreed upon by the evaluating team was, "What impact does participation in this literacy program have on the learners?" The quantitative component was based on achievement in reading and writing skills. The qualitative component allowed the evaluators to discover "the meaning and impact of the program through the perspective of the participants" (p. ii). The result was a study that "illuminated the internal process and dynamics" of the program (p. 14).

Homeless literacy projects cannot fully have their picture taken, so to speak, by quantitative outcome studies alone (Mitroff, 1983). Barriers to meaningful evaluations that focus on outcomes include brief time in class, frequent resident movement among shelter programs, a constantly changing education program, and time constraints on instructors. Evaluation should include qualitative approaches which focus on the impact of participation on learners. Marshall and Rossman (1989) point out that "it is essential in the study of people to know just how people define the situation in which they find themselves" (p. 46).

Assessing what is occurring currently is one evaluation approach; another is assessing what happens over time as in a process or follow up study. Darkenwald and Valentine (1985) see the goal of adult basic education follow up studies as attainment of "valid, reliable, and generalizable data with respect to a broad array of outcomes or changes that can be attributed to program participation" (p. 17). They point out the difficulty in conducting follow up studies, including the requirement to detect change over time and reasonably generalize that the changes are due to participation in the program.

Attempting follow up studies with homeless adults would be especially difficult given the transient nature of the population. Response rates might be unacceptably low. However, since most homeless adults stay in the same area where they experience homelessness (Bassuk, 1990; Children's Defense Fund, 1991; Dail, 1990; Goodman, 1991; Hagen, 1987), a follow up study could be designed to yield data that illuminates program effectiveness.

Knowles (1980) points out that informal evaluation is going on constantly in adult education programs. Participants provide ongoing feedback via their comments and actions; they provide data, as well, by not coming back to classes. In addition, instructors are continually assessing how well lessons are progressing and making immediate adjustments to the sessions. However,

Knowles observes, "this continuous but almost unconscious evaluation results in many on-the-spot improvements. . . . But it does not serve the same purpose as periodic, systematically planned evaluations" (p. 203).

The use of informal evaluation techniques such as portfolios containing evidence of learning for each participant is a step beyond intuition and serves the dual purpose of informing both the learner and the program of progress. Combining the intuitive and informal approaches with quantitative and qualitative procedures will help program planners understand both the processes and long-term impacts of participation.

DISCUSSION

Homeless people are on the receiving end of many programs ostensibly designed to help them overcome their crisis circumstances. If literacy education is to be part of the longer term solutions for helping adults leave and not return to homelessness, the programs must be thoughtfully planned, administered, and evaluated. The most important evaluator will be the learner (Chavis, Stucky, & Wandersman, 1983) who may be entering the program with much enthusiasm and leaving with few documented results.

CHAPTER 8

Issues and Implications

Given the predicted increase in homelessness in the United States, particularly for women with children, there will be no shortage of opportunities for adult basic education professionals to serve this special population. During the first three years of the McKinney-funded adult education programs, over 70,000 people were served (U.S. Department of Education, 1992). Obscured by the numbers, however, are the difficult issues demanding attention and the implications for future efforts. These issues and implications will be briefly discussed, followed by suggestions for the ongoing homeless adult education enterprise.

ISSUES

Some of the issues encountered by homeless literacy project staff have been a carryover from the larger ABE programs. Others are particularly related to ABE efforts with homeless adult learners. Ambiguous instructional objectives for those learners who are not illiterate but who are lacking in the skills needed to pass the GED examinations have long been a concern in adult basic education. Several prominent researchers in literacy education have focused on nonreader concerns (Fingeret, 1989; Harman, 1987; Beder, 1991) and have shed new light on appropriate attitudes and instructional strategies. ABE programs have struggled to offer appropriate instruction to those adults who have basic literacy skills or functional literacy levels but would need lengthy preparation for a high school equivalency certificate.

It is in this middle ground that lifeskills and competency-based approaches have proliferated. Considerable emphasis is placed on learner-demonstrated competencies, although not necessarily learner-selected competencies. In many instances, these competencies are intricately tied to program evaluation. It is little wonder that "high mobility of clients" and "the nature of student involvement" continue to be reported as barriers to instruction in McKinney education programs (U.S. Department of Education, 1992). Demonstrating competencies takes time as does selecting competencies that are relevant to homeless adult learners.

The need for shelter provider support and for managing poor learning environments are two issues particular to homeless adult education. Both concerns appear in the U.S. Department of Education's 1992 report as barriers to instruction, just as they did in the initial project reports (U.S. Department of Education, 1990a). The regular literacy programs are typically guests in some other organization's space since literacy classes are usually scattered around a community. But little in that experience prepared program planners and instructors for dealing with homeless shelter staff, philosophy, and environment. Homeless literacy program developers can not assume shelter provider support or understanding of program goals. Shelter staff goals and operating philosophies are not necessarily educator goals and philosophies. Educators will always be challenged to fit into homeless environments while maintaining educational goals.

Instructors used to setting up classes in local schools, public libraries, churches, community centers, and community colleges take dealing with keys, space in someone else's desk, and "day teacher" complaints about "night class messes" in their stride. But the instructor is still in charge of the learning environment during instructional time. This control is often given up, or barely maintained, in shelter environments. Little reason exists to expect improvements in the homeless shelter instructional environments or the environments at related locations, unless facilities are being constructed from scratch and designed to accommodate educational programs. Literacy program designers will have to continue seeking "environment-proof" teaching methods or alternative sites located away from homeless living quarters.

Another concern is that taking adult basic education programs to homeless adults also involves dealing with the psychological trauma of homelessness itself and the trauma that often precedes homelessness. By operating onsite, literally in living rooms, kitchens, and bedrooms, instructors are going to be encountering women who have just that day or week left an abusive situation (Shinn, Knickman, & Weitzman, 1991). Other homeless adults may be withdrawn, depressed, or agitated. While the focus of this book has been on the homeless adult as a learner rather than as a member of a particular subgroup, program planners and instructors will have to deal with a wide range of learner difficulties associated with mental illness, substance or alcohol abuse, and psychological trauma (Breakey & Fischer, 1990; Toro, Trickett, Wall, & Salem, 1991). Instructors in the broader ABE programs have faced these difficulties, but hardly to this extent.

Finally, high attrition rates are often a way of life in ABE programs in general but are literally built into the homeless adult education efforts. Instructors may be dealing with a different set of learners from one evening to the next; however, in transitional programs some adults may be involved in instruction that promises to be more long-term than is possible in emergency shelters. It is not unusual, however, for transitional shelter residents to leave the shelter program upon acquiring a job, or perhaps even without acquiring employment. In 1989–1990 over nine thousand students were reported as having left a shelter before completing instruction (U.S. Department of Education, 1992). This mobility keeps constant pressure on program planners and stress on instructors who will likely witness only limited educational progress at a particular site.

FUTURE CONCERNS

Future areas of concern can be thought of in five broad categories: learning environments, time, curriculum, program administration, and community partnerships. These areas will be discussed and strategies offered.

Environment

Literacy education for homeless adults cannot be considered in isolation from the environment in which it is taking place. The environment includes the physical circumstances, the clientele, and the shelter staff and philosophy. If educators find they can best reach homeless adults by establishing literacy programs onsite, they will have to continue seeking ways to either reduce the environmental stresses or capitalize on them. Examples include using an external diploma approach* or employing educational technology that allows learners some degree of privacy within a public situation. Although offsite class locations present many administrative problems, they may result in a better learning environment.

Shelter provider support makes a significant difference in educational outcomes for learners. Program planners and instructors will have to maintain ongoing communication between themselves and those who operate shelters and related services. A major program limitation reported after the second year of the McKinney-funded literacy initiatives was "apathy of shelter staff, which led to scheduling conflicts and lack of encouragement to students to attend" (U.S. Department of Education, 1992). Designing programs that demonstrate to the providers the benefits of participation will continue to be a challenge for program planners.

Time

Literacy programs for the homeless are driven not only by environment but by time. The time a learner will have to participate in instruction largely defines the possibilities. Educators have been recommending since the first reports about the McKinney-funded education initiatives that homeless adults have more stable and long-term residential circumstances (U.S. Department of Education, 1990a). However, the reality is likely to

---

*Board of Cooperative Educational Services, #3, External Diploma Program, Adult Career Center, 17 Westminster Ave., Dix Hills, New York, 11746–6399.

be more of the status quo, and educators will have to focus on strategies to expand the net of influence or contact in spite of brief program participation.

Rather than viewing a learner's participation as a short-term event, program planners can work to broaden the instructional net. The initial contact with learners can, at the very least, be supplemented by referrals and by personal intervention and followthrough at the highest level. Programs can be designed to involve learners in community activities or bring the community to them. Learners can be informed immediately of other class sites in the area and encouraged to attend them concurrent with their shelter stay or after leaving the shelter. Shelter providers and volunteers can be enlisted to help residents attend nearby educational programs.

Curriculum

Both the second and the third year federal reports on the McKinney education projects revealed difficulties with curriculum selection and utilization. "Use of irrelevant curriculum," "pre-selected curriculum which did not meet student needs," and "initial use of an academic curriculum" are listed as program limitations (U.S. Department of Education, 1992, pp. 6–7). The call for novel and creative approaches to basic skills instruction rings loudly for all literacy programs, but especially so for the homeless literacy projects.

While most programs are trying, with the limited financial resources, to serve a wide spread of educational needs, an alternative consideration might be to focus on one instructional area. An example would be focusing on GED preparation. The process of studying for, practicing for, and actually taking the examination is lengthy and difficult. Arranging for transportation, time off from work, child care, and payment of testing fee requires considerable endurance and support. Homeless adults may need someone to go with them to a testing site and to help negotiate the process or simply provide moral support.

While acquisition of the GED is no guarantee of escape from homelessness, it is a significant and concrete accomplishment that cannot be taken away from the homeless adult. In 1989 and 1990, 1,591 homeless adults acquired the GED or some other type of secondary diploma (U.S. Department of Education, 1992). This represents a tiny portion of the 70,000 adults served. Trying to serve as many adults as possible has often brought frustrating results, and a GED focus option might be a viable alternative. Another example would be to focus on beginning reading and math instruction.

Administration

It will be very difficult to serve homeless adults efficiently and creatively when ABE program administrators are holding the homeless projects up to the same bureaucratic requirements of the regular program. Program participants often require considerable one-to-one attention and may not work in groups. They may also require some intervention beyond the standard classroom expectations of the teacher. In addition, instructors working with transitional programs which use the integrated model of literacy education will be expected to spend additional time in staff meetings and planning sessions.

Innovations are quickly stifled when attendance requirements force cancellation of programs. The ABE program in general has suffered for years because of funding formulas that focus on attendance and subsequent budget dollars. The work to be completed cannot be adequately done with homeless adults if instructors are not allowed to weather ups and downs in shelter attendance, shifts in shelter staff, and the trust-building component that simply takes time. Program administrators should be encouraged to allow for considerable leeway when the learners are homeless.

Community Partnerships

Literacy programs have historically stood alone, with the need for literacy skills treated as a separate entity from other needs. However, educators working with homeless adults have seen how literacy skills have to be connected to other life needs. Basic skills education on its own is unlikely to have a lasting impact on homelessness itself and may have limited impact on individual participants (Fingeret & Danin, 1991; Fox, 1986).

A broader view has literacy educators, shelter providers, other service providers, volunteers, and learners working together to design a coordinated system of educational support. Fox (1986) makes a distinction between individually oriented and community-oriented literacy programs. Fox asserts that the community-oriented program places "emphasis on dealing with the person within the community," (p. 16) which leads to broader programming such as parenting education and career counseling.

A community-oriented approach could foster referral centers, advocacy activities, and a support base for persons leaving homelessness. Fox recommends a program model that would function as a literacy support program. "It should be in the form of a literacy resource and assistance center that would, first, address literacy-related needs, whatever they are" (p. 13). Fox envisions readers being available to assist adults with whatever they believe they need. In many ways, literacy instructors located in shelters are already using this approach to assisting homeless adults. The concept can be applied to community locations as well.

Ideally, whether the resource and assistance is a center in place or in concept, people other than literacy instructors should be involved. Shelter providers, other service providers, volunteers, community agency staff, and others who come in contact with homeless people can be trained to promote learning when their respective clients are involved in literacy tasks. Rather than seeing literacy as a separate issue and referring people to literacy classes, community resource persons can support literacy activities themselves. They may help clients read and comprehend eviction notices, teach them coping skills that will help in the management of benefits payments and requirements, or explain the process involved in locating child care.

Members of the community can become involved in the

education of those homeless adults whose lack of basic skills makes their transition out of homelessness especially difficult. They can also continue to provide support so that adults can maintain new living arrangements and not return to shelters. These community literacy supporters will be part of "expanding the net" of education discussed earlier.

RESEARCH

Expanded concepts of literacy education became necessary when literacy program coordinators and instructors made their way into homeless shelters, soup kitchens, and advocacy organizations. Likewise, contributions from other educational and psychological fields have filtered into the knowledge base that supports literacy instructors' work with homeless adults. The ecological analogy and environment-centered as opposed to individual deficit model of understanding homelessness was contributed by community psychology (Toro, Trickett, Wall, & Salem, 1991). Social support systems, social buffering, and the effect of loss of home came from social psychology and sociology (Rivlin, 1990; Rivlin & Imbimbo, 1989).

Qualitative and ethnographic research are much needed in the field of homeless research. Studies in the uniqueness of homeless adult learners is sorely needed from which further program designs and curriculum materials can be developed. Field studies, longitudinal studies, and participatory action research is called for to advance understanding about the world of the homeless adult and family as well as of homeless learners.

Adult basic education programs for homeless adults can no more be isolated from other disciplines than from the communities and environments in which homeless adults are attempting to meet their educational goals. Literacy projects are in prime locations to contribute to the knowledge base about adult learners and homelessness and to interact with researchers in psychology, sociology, and adult education on common research issues. Shinn, Knickman, and Weitzman (1991) and Sosin, Piliavin, and Westerfelt (1990) have demonstrated the complexity of homelessness and the research methodology necessary to meet this complexity. Homeless literacy educators can contribute much needed research as a natural consequence of their daily work and interaction with homeless adults who have immediate needs for skills.

Literacy education is just one part of the support that homeless people need, and it will likely have limited impact on the problems of homelessness if it attempts to stand on its own. At their best, adult basic education administrators, instructors, and volunteers serve as connectors, coordinators, creators, and natural researchers. These qualities, when applied to literacy education for homeless adults, can lead to positive outcomes for both learners and their communities.

REFERENCES

Bassuk, E. L. (1990). Who are the homeless families? Characteristics of sheltered mothers and children. *Community Mental Health Journal, 26*(5), 425–434.

Bassuk, E. L., & Rosenberg, L. (1988). Why does family homelessness occur? A case-control study. *American Journal of Public Health, 48*(7), 783–788.

Beder, H. (1991). The stigma of illiteracy. *Adult Basic Education, 1*(2), 67–78.

Beder, H., & Valentine, T. (1987). *Iowa's adult basic education students: Descriptive profiles based on motivations, cognitive ability, and sociodemographic statistics.* Des Moines, IA: Iowa Department of Education.

Berlin, G., & Sum, A. (1988). *Toward a more perfect union: Basic skills, poor families and our economic future.* New York: Ford Foundation.

Boraks, N. (1988). Balancing adult literacy research and program evaluation. *Adult Literacy and Basic Education, 12*(2), 66–77.

Breakey, W. R., & Fischer, P. J. (1990). Homelessness: The extent of the problem. *Journal of Social Issues, 46*(4), 31–47.

Camperell, K., Rachal, J., & Pierce, W. L. (1983). ABE/GED teachers: Characteristics and training needs. *Adult Literacy and Basic Education, 7*(2), 77–85.

Caplan, W., & Nelson, S. D. (1973). On being useful: The nature and consequences of psychological research on social problems. *American Psychologist, 28*, 199–211.

Chavis, D. M., Stucky, P. E., & Wandersman, A. (1983). Returning basic research to the community. *American Psychologist, 38*, 424–434.

Children's Defense Fund. (1991). *Homeless families: Failed policies and young victims.* Washington, DC: Author.

Cohen, M. B. (1989). Social work practice with homeless mentally ill people: Engaging the client. *Social Work, 34*(6), 505–508.

Coles, G. (1983–84). Adult illiteracy and learning theory: A study of cognition and activity. *Science and Society, 47*(4), 451–482.

Comprehensive Adult Student Assessment System. (1990). *Adult education for the homeless: 1990 report.* San Diego, CA: Author.

Comprehensive Adult Student Assessment System. (1991). *Adult education for the homeless: 1991 report.* San Diego, CA: Author.

Dail, P. W. (1990). The psychosocial context of homeless mothers with young children: Program and policy implications. *Child Welfare, 69*(4), 291–307.

Darkenwald, G., & Valentine, T. (1985). Outcomes of participation in adult basic education. *Lifelong Learning, 8*(5), 17–22.

Dluhy, M. J. (1990). Community perceptions of the homeless: Factors in intervention strategies with the homeless. *Social Work Research and Abstracts, 26*(1), 18–24.

Drake, R., Osher, F., & Wallach, M. (1991). Homelessness and dual diagnosis. *American Psychologist, 46*(11), 1149–1158.

Egan, G. (1984). People in systems: A comprehensive model for psychosocial education and training. In D. Larson (Ed.), *Teaching psychological skills: Models for giving psychology away* (pp. 21–43). Monterey, CA: Brooks/Cole.

Fellenz, R. A., et al. (1981). *Individual development and adult basic education: A student followup.* (Report No. CE-030–532). Houston, TX: Texas A.& M. University, Texas Education Agency, Division of Adult and Continuing Education. (ERIC Document Reproduction Service No. ED 210 436)

Fingeret, A. (1985). *North Carolina adult basic education instructional program evaluation, 1985.* Raleigh, NC: Department of Adult and Community Education, North Carolina State University.

Fingeret, H. (1989). The social and historical context of participatory literacy education. In H. Fingeret & P. Jurmo (Eds.), *Participatory literacy education* (pp. 5–15). New Directions for Continuing Education, no. 42. San Francisco: Jossey-Bass.

Fingeret, H. (1990). Changing literacy instruction: Moving beyond the status quo. In F. Chisman & Associates (Eds.) *Leadership for literacy* (pp. 25–50). San Francisco: Jossey-Bass.

Fingeret, H. (1991). Meaning, experience, and literacy. *Adult Basic Education, 1*(1), 4–11.

Fingeret, H., & Danin, S. (1991, January). *They really put a hurtin' on my brain: Learning in Literacy Volunteers of New York City (Executive Summary)*. Durham, NC: Literacy South.

Fischer, J. K., & Evanson, J. I. (1979). Test scores don't tell the whole story. In A. B. Knox (Ed.), *Assessing the impact of continuing education* (pp. 29–36). New Directions for Continuing Education, no. 3. San Francisco: Jossey-Bass.

Fox, M. (1986). *A look at illiteracy in America today: The problem, the solution, the alternatives*. Washington, DC: Push Literacy Action Now.

Fried, M. (1963). Grieving for a lost home. In L. J. Duhl (Ed.), *The urban condition* (pp. 151–171). New York: Basic Books.

Galbraith, M. W. (1991). The adult learning transactional process. In M. W. Galbraith (Ed.), *Facilitating adult learning: A transactional process* (pp. 1–32). Malabar, FL: Krieger.

General Accounting Office, Comptroller General of the U.S. (1988, April). *Homeless mentally ill: Problems and options in estimating numbers and trends. Report to the Chairman, Committee on Labor and Human Resources, U.S. Senate* (Report No. GAO/PEMO-88–24). Washington DC: General Accounting Office. (ERIC Document Reproduction Service No. Ed 302 738).

Goodman, L. (1991). The relationship between social support and family homelessness: A comparison study of homeless and housed mothers. *Journal of Community Psychology, 19*, 321–332.

Goodman, L., Saxe, L., & Harvey, M. (1991). Homelessness as psychological trauma. *American Psychologist, 46*(11), 1219–1225.

Hagen, J. L. (1987). Gender and homelessness. *Social Work, 32*(4), 312–316.

Harman, D. (1987). *Illiteracy: A national dilemma*. New York: Cambridge.

Hollingsworth, D., Craven, J., Morris, N., Parker, C., Rainey, O., & Payne, G. (1990). *A proposal for a case management system for the homeless population*. Raleigh, NC: Department of Human Resources.

Hunter, C., & Harman, D. (1979). *Adult illiteracy in the United States: A report to the Ford Foundation*. New York: McGraw-Hill.

Hutchison, W. J., Searight, P., & Stretch, J. J. (1986). Multidimensional networking: A response to the needs of homeless families. *Social Work, 31*(6), 427–429.

Imbimbo, J., & Pfeffer, R. (1987). Reflections of home: Women in shelters. *Women and Environments, 10*(1), 14–15.

Interagency Council on the Homeless. (1990). *Fact sheet series: Series 1–5.* Washington, D.C.: Author.

Johnson, A. K., & Kreuger, L. W. (1989). Toward a better understanding of homeless women. *Social Work, 34*(6), 537–540.

Jurmo, P. (1989a). The case for participatory literacy education. In H. Fingeret & P. Jurmo (Eds.), *Participatory literacy education* (pp. 17–28). New Directions for Continuing Education, no. 42. San Francisco: Jossey-Bass.

Jurmo, P. (1989b). Instruction and management: Where participatory theory is put into practice. In H. Fingeret & P. Jurmo (Eds.), *Participatory literacy education* (pp. 29–34). New Directions for Continuing Education, no. 42. San Francisco: Jossey-Bass.

Kansas State Board of Education. (1991). *Adult performance parenting literacy experiences.* Topeka, KS: Author.

Kazemek, F. E. (1983). An examination of the adult performance level project and its effects upon adult literacy education in the United States. *Viewpoints*, (120), pp. 1–26. (ERIC Document Reproductions Services No. Ed 236 576)

Kazemek, F. E. (1984). Adult literacy education: An ethical endeavor. *Adult Literacy and Basic Education, 8*(2), 61–72.

Kazemek, F. E. (1985). Functional literacy is not enough: Adult literacy as a developmental process. *Journal of Reading, 28*(4), 332–335.

Knowles, M. S. (1970). *The modern practice of adult education: Andragogy versus pedagogy.* New York: Association Press.

Knowles, M. S. (1980). *The modern practice of adult education: Pedagogy to andragogy* (revised and updated). New York: Cambridge.

Koegel, P., Burnam, M. A., & Farr, R. K. (1990). Subsistence adaptation among homeless adults in the inner city of Los Angeles. *Journal of Social Issues, 46*(4), 83–107.

Kozol, J. (1988). *Rachel and her children.* New York: Fawcett Columbine.

Langer, J. A. (1986). *A sociocognitive perspective on literacy.* (Report No. CS-210–097). *Viewpoints*, (120), pp. 1–38. (ERIC Document Reproduction Service No. Ed 274 988)

Levine, I. S., & Rog, D. J. (1990). Mental health services for homeless mentally ill persons: Federal initiatives and current service trends. *American Psychologist, 45*(8), 963–968.

Marlowe, M., Branson, R., Childress, W., & Parker, G. (1991). Adult basic skills instruction training and experiential learning theory. *Adult Basic Education, 1*(3), 155–167.

Marshall, C., & Rossman, G. B. (1989). *Designing qualitative research*. Newbury Park, CA: Sage.

Maslow, A. H. (1970). *Motivation and personality*. New York: Harper & Row.

McChesney, K. Y. (1990). Family homelessness: A systemic problem. *Journal of Social Issues, 46*(4), 191–205.

Milburn, N., & D'Ercole, A. (1991). Homeless women: Moving toward a comprehensive model. *American Psychologist, 46*(11), 1161–1169.

Mitroff, I. I. (1983). Beyond experimentation: New methods for a new age. In E. Seidman (Ed.), *Handbook of social intervention* (pp. 163–177). Beverly Hills, CA: Sage.

Mowbray, C. T. (1985). Homelessness in America: Myths and realities. *American Journal of Orthopsychiatry, 55*(1), 4–8.

National Coalition for the Homeless. (1991). *Homelessness in America: A summary*. Washington, D.C.: Author.

Padak, N. D., & Padak, G. M. (1991). What works: Adult literacy program evaluation. *Journal of Reading, 34*(5), 374–379.

Pardeck, J. T. (1990). An analysis of the deep social structure preventing the development of a national policy for children and families in the United States. *Early Child Development and Care, 57*, 23–30.

Rivlin, L. G. (1990). The significance of home and homelessness. *Marriage and Family Review, 15*(1–2), 39–56.

Rivlin, L. G., & Imbimbo, J. (1989). Self-help efforts in a squatter community: Implications for addressing contemporary homelessness. *American Journal of Community Psychology, 17*(6), 705–728.

Ropers, R. H. (1988). *The invisible homeless: A new urban ecology*. New York: Human Sciences Press.

Rossi, P. H. (1990). The old homeless and the new homeless in historical perspective. *American Psychologist, 45*(8), 954–959.

Russell, B. G. (1988). Silent sisters: An ethnography of homeless women in Baltimore, Maryland (Doctoral dissertation, University of Maryland, 1988). *Dissertation Abstracts International, 49*, 2282.

Ryan, W. (1971). *Blaming the victim*. New York: Random.

Shinn, M. (1991, August). *Homelessness: What is a psychologist to do?* Presidential address to the Society for Community Research and Action at the annual meeting of the American Psychological Association, San Francisco, CA.

Shinn, M., Knickman, J. R., & Weitzman, B.C. (1991). Social relationships and vulnerability to becoming homeless among poor families. *American Psychologist, 46*(11), 1180–1187.

Sosin, M. R., & Grossman, S. (1991). The mental health system and the etiology of homelessness: A comparison study. *Journal of Community Psychology, 19*(4), 337–350.

Sosin, M. R., Piliavin, I., & Westerfelt, H. (1990). Toward a longitudinal analysis of homelessness. *Journal of Social Issues, 46*(4), 157–174.

Sticht, T. (1987). Literacy, cognitive robotics, and general technology training for marginally literate adults. In D. Wagner (Ed.), *The future of literacy in a changing world* (pp. 289–301). Oxford: Pergamon.

Stoner, M. R. (1988). Beyond shelter: Policy directions for the prevention of homelessness. *Social Work Research and Abstracts, 25*(4), 7–11.

Stuart, J. (1990). *Lifeskills for the homeless curriculum*. Raleigh, NC: Wake Technical Community College.

Toro, P. A., Trickett, E. J., Wall, D. D., & Salem, D. A. (1991). Homelessness in the United States: An ecological perspective. *American Psychologist, 46*(11), 1208–1218.

University of the State of New York. (1990). *Literacy training for the homeless: Guidelines for effective programs*. Albany: NY State Education Department.

U.S. Department of Education. (1988). *Stewart B. McKinney homeless assistance act (PL 100–177): Adult education for the homeless*. (Report No. CFDA-84.192). Washington, DC: Government Printing Office.

U.S. Department of Education. (1989). *Adult education for the homeless: FY 1989 project abstracts*. Washington, DC: U.S. Government Printing Office.

U.S. Department of Education. (1990a). *Profiles of state programs: Adult education for the homeless*. Washington, DC: U.S. Government Printing Office.

U.S. Department of Education. (1990b). *Education for homeless adults: The first year.* Washington, DC: U.S. Government Printing Office.

U.S. Department of Education. (1992, February). *Education for homeless adults: The 1989–1990 report.* Washington, DC: U.S. Government Printing Office.

Vella J. (1989). *Learning to teach.* New York: Save the Children.

Walsh, M. E. (1990, August). Psychosocial functioning in homeless and poor housed families. In Y. Rafferty (Chair), *Public interest miniconvention—homelessness: Community research, action, and agenda for public policy.* Symposium conducted at the 98th Annual Meeting of the American Psychological Association, Boston, MA.

Weber, R. (1975). Adult illiteracy in the United States. In J. B. Carroll & Chall, J. S. (Eds.), *Toward a literate society: The report of the committee on reading of the National Academy of Education* (pp. 147–164). New York: McGraw-Hill.

Willing, D. C. (1989). Program evaluation as a strategy for program improvement in adult basic education. *Lifelong Learning, 12*(4), 4–9.

Wood, D., Valdez, R. B., Hayashi, T., & Shen, A. (1990). Homeless and housed families in Los Angeles: A study comparing demographic, economic, and family function characteristics. *American Journal of Public Health, 80*(9), 1049–1052.

Wright, J. D., & Weber, E. (1987). *Homelessness and health.* New York: McGraw-Hill.

INDEX